JOURNEY PROUD

JOURNEY PROUD

Southern Women's Personal Writings

Collected and
Introduced by
Agnes
McDonald

CAROLINA WREN PRESS
Durham, North Carolina

Funding for this publication was made in part by the Durham Arts Council and the North Carolina Arts Council and the Mary Duke Biddle Foundation.

A portion of the Introduction appeared in a somewhat different form in "The Arts Journal" December 1990.

ISBN 0-932112-36-6

Library of Congress Cataloging-in-Publication Data
Journey proud : Southern women's personal writings /
collected and introduced by Agnes McDonald.
p.   cm.
ISBN 0-932112-36-6 (pbk.) : $10.95
1. American prose literature—Southern States.   2. American prose literature—Women authors.   3. Women—Southern States—Diaries.   4. Diaries—Women authors.
I. McDonald, Agnes, 1932-
PS551.J68   1994   94-10563
818'.54080804—dc20   CIP

Carolina Wren Press thanks the following volunteers for their help:
Editing by Shelley Day, Charlotte Hoffman and Ruth Smullin
Manuscript entry by Shelley Day
Copyediting by Betty Hodges and Tammi Brooks
Proofreading by Elaine Goolsby and Maria Lee
Book design by Martha Scotford
Cover design by Martha Scotford and William C. Massey

Manufactured in the USA.
Carolina Wren Press
120 Morris Street
Durham, North Carolina 27701

I gratefully acknowledge the help, the encouragement, the patience and the shared visions of the many people who urged me on with this book. I wish to thank specifically the teachers in the North Carolina Writing Project, who first convinced me with the power of their words; Weymouth Center, where much of this book was revised; Mab Segrest, for her valuable association in the beginning; Nancy Markham, whose discernment and high standards regarding the journal itself set a mark to which I could aspire; Martha MacLennan and Sue Headrick, for their careful and sensitive handling of the text as if it were a living thing and for their typing, word processing and proofreading along the way, which created in me a sense that all was well. I would have been a child lost in the woods of words, had it not been for the readings of the manuscript by Susan Ketchin and Mel McLaurin, who made it possible for me to start to see the trees. My thanks also to the women, whose writing appears in this collection, who waited and kept the faith.

—Agnes McDonald

This book is dedicated to
all women
who have let us hear their voices,
and to
every woman
who has yet to be heard.

TABLE OF CONTENTS

INTRODUCTION | Agnes McDonald

In writing this introduction, I have turned instinctively to story and to my grandmother, Esther Morton Baptist, of Ivy Depot, Virginia. Ivy was a stop on the railroad with a general store and a post office, about seven miles from Charlottesville. My grandmother lived in several other places as the years wore on, but it is this Ivy grandmother that I remember most vividly, and Ivy Depot is the focus of the story I want to tell.

"Ama," as we called her, was the wife of a country doctor and the mother of six children. That is, part of her was. Another part sought beauty and order and self-expression in hymns played on an out-of-tune piano, poetry, her flower garden, handwork and hats. She delighted in hats, buying them, wearing them. She looked good in hats and she knew it.

Like many farm women of meager means, she became a child again at the prospect of a trip to town, to relatives in a nearby village, or to friends in another county. A trip like this could awaken her at three a.m. wide-eyed with anticipation, turgid with energy. She would throw off the remnants of sleep to check her preparations for the hundredth time, to fry chicken on the wood stove, make deviled eggs and cucumber sandwiches—cucumbers sliced paper thin, home-baked bread and hand-churned butter. I'll never forget the smell of all of this wrapped in waxed paper, enough of everything for a tribal vision quest in the outback. Too much, I always thought, but somehow her fixings were always eaten.

And, of course, at the other end of the trip, eager to savor every minute no matter the hour, she found herself paying for her early rising and the energy sapped along the way by several arguments with Granddaddy. She would say, finally giving in reluctantly, "I guess I just didn't sleep much last night. Journey proud, you know."

As women prepare for another sort of journey, journal writing takes place during what time we steal or what is stolen for us by circumstance or adrenalin's rush, in anticipation of a journey on which we are about to embark. Although we are not literally "going somewhere," we may be just as exuberant about the journeys of our lives, enough to care deeply about recording and reflecting. So we are, in every sense, journey proud.

Journals, unlike memoirs and autobiography, are characteristically written in the present about the present, a melting snowflake on the window between the past and the future. We write in our diaries or journals as my Ama made cucumber sandwiches—it is something to do while we wait, something we can touch and taste, ensuring that we will be nourished, a creation with our own stamp on it, words to take with us, something from home.

Each woman has her story. Not the one defined and authorized by the majority culture, but the story she and her journal know. These stories are not the fairy tales of romance and handsome princes. Nor are they the myths of security and protection many women found out too late were lies, or at least costly trades. What, then, are the real stories?

Seldom are women's private lives voiced in public, even now, in this time of screaming tabloids and encounter groups. The stiff upper lip is best and she who keeps her own counsel is the one who wins the prize. But the facade falls away in times of grief or exhaustion, fear or desperation. The truth is alluded to in jokes women laugh at together over canning, folding laundry, or passing each other in the ladies' room at work. Unified by their silences, these women of the past still exist, isolated from anyone who will listen, invisible to all but our journals.

"Mens is a strange nation unto theirselves," said an old woman who used to care for me, hers a story in one sentence. You could see their stories in the ways their eyes flared, or in the way they brushed away errant strands of hair from their faces. My mother used to get the mop out after everyone had gone to bed and tell her story to the kitchen floor. And all we ever knew was the linger of bleach in the morning at breakfast. So women have told their stories with their bodies, writing them down in their journals with hands. The journal has been, as someone said, a woman's flesh made word.

In collecting and studying journals of women who consider themselves southern, I have observed not so much southern women generally, but many women's lives individually recorded. These are lives termed ordinary by some and certainly not public lives of fame or vast influence, but they are extraordinary in their own ways. These women artists, teachers, poets, and students are not writing as mothers, daughters, and wives of historically significant males. Journal stories have a far different and greater value than simply records of the intimate side of life with the senator. We, who in our journals have tracked our own lives for centuries, find meaning in naming our own experience, in naming our world. We write; we read what we write. We piece our lives together on the page like scraps for patchwork quilts. Many of us write solely for ourselves, never expecting or wanting to be read, though some write for future generations.

I have developed strong bonds with these women who keep journals, a sometimes soul-wrenching activity when carried beyond the level of the red leather five-year diary which many of us kept as girls. I have wanted to see what the threads are that run through these journals, our own versions of the days of our lives, lives blurred by expectations, myth, illusion. For women in this collection, the journal is the threshing floor where agonies and joys are brought to be beaten husk from grain, to be taken down to essence. We have wanted to still the babble and listen more deeply to our own voices.

What do we write about? We write of the family, that peculiarly southern attachment, a part of our lives rarely ignored in our journals. Family relationships are not always easy, yet few women sent material from their journals that dealt with the violent and turbulent side of relationships. Dirty linen, possibly. But the decline or death of parents looms large as a subject of intense daily exploration, painful as the daughter comes to terms with old unresolved issues, her own mortality, and loss. In "Death Details," for example, Jane Hanudel writes of her father's final illness and, equally important, her mother's stoic resignation in fulfilling her duties as caretaker and widow.

Small comforts, habits, rituals, sights and sounds are strong elements in our journals, especially those of Joy Averett, a teacher from Oxford, North Carolina, and Gwynne Hackworth, writing of a Florida childhood:

"I remember saddle shoes and cigarettes, riding around in my old blue car drinking beer with the girls, Trail's End, and Tina's birthday. JV and summers, and ashes falling from the sky. Halloween and jumping on the streets. I remember the orange grove behind the house and the beatnik. I remember the Farrell's station wagon with curtains. And kindergarten—riding in the carpool. I remember popcorn at Granddad's and swimming, feeling the mud squish up between my toes. And sometimes a sharp object, metal, brick or trash. And swimming out too far. And fishing at Mr. Miller's. I remember playing in the orange groves and walking all the way around them on the roads. And being afraid of snakes and bears. And feeling so alone, vulnerable. And roses and strawberries."

A sense of location, its furnishings and our reaction to these, pleasant or unpleasant, makes of the scene and the weather a barometer of our interior "weather." Like May Sarton, we southern journal writers often begin our writing with what we see as we survey the room or look through the window. "Now there are no footprints on my day," one woman writes. Pages sparkle with sensuous detail: the fall of snow through pines; the taste of raspberries; the strange, wild taste of poke; the memories of the smoke-filled bedroom of a mother now dying of lung cancer.

But journal writers reveal the southern scene to be more than snowfalls and the smell of gingerbread, old folks and the gathering of herbs. There is sadness as these pass and a hope to keep these treasures from disappearing by writing them down. There is a "bittersweet romantic ambivalence for these old ways, and for what is true and just for everyone," Jacklyn Potter writes in a letter about her journals. There is great love, yes, and pride. But there is also anger and disgust with sexism, racism, class barriers, poverty, and towns and minds with two faces. And a determination to change things.

Kendall writes:

"Thought how much I hate the whiteness of this city; how far away the black folks live from the whites, how far away the black world is from these rich students with their cars and condos. How I ache for greens and cornbread and black laughter and gospel. How pale the white world is, cradled in wealth and protected from life by dollar bills. I think when I leave here I will go to Washington, D. C. and teach in an urban college. Or Chicago. If they will have me. Somewhere there are old women, like me, struggling to know something with life under their belts and children hanging off their arms. I will leave the white Texas world behind me, glad of what I got from it, glad of what I gave, but knowing Texas is not the South."

At home and in the world, we face conflicts with the status quo, with traditional roles, with expectations, some to be embraced, some to be considered and rejected. The woman who struggles to find and demand a "room of her own" may be asking for psychic space rather than physical space. She struggles for acceptance at work and is outraged at the "way things are," expecting more, trying to be more for herself and using her journal to define herself in a sea of demands. The journal seems a center in the eye of this storm. Betty Hodges uses her journal to document her juggling of many roles.

"My Timex watch strap doesn't have a right notch: one is too loose, another too tight. It's like home and work for me as a woman. There's no right place. I have to have both."

We write in the pages of the journal of love, the comfort of friends, relationships, or the loss of these. Sometimes it becomes so painful that we must move on to other subjects in the interest of self-preservation.

Southern women are funny, with an irreverent sense of humor, and, at the same time, we are dead serious. We are tired of waiting. Impatience is one of the predominant subjects of these journals. Sue Inman deplores waiting, and particularly waiting for men to meet the challenge of the "new" woman.

Who are we, living in no particular moment, and where are we going? And what will we take with us? Certainly the journal, and the example of other strong southern women. Judy Hogan compares the bittersweet taste of poke with what it means to be a southern woman, "Maybe I do live in the South because of the poke. Not just the poke, but it's a kind of symbol. Cresses are another. I don't really fit in any one culture, or in any one place. I'm loose now, in a way, of all social conventions. Inside, which is where it matters. If I want to go gather poke, here at 9 o'clock Saturday morning, no one will stop me."

Although we use our journals in different ways and for different reasons, writing serves us well through periods of questioning, reminiscing, spiritual searching and decision-making. The journal, and whatever may come of it, be it creative product or self-understanding, is a talk with ourselves, "a glimpse," as Jacklyn Potter writes, "like a round crevice in Magritte's sky."

VOICES THAT SOUND LIKE HOME

Sometimes it is the same voice that speaks in my other writing. Sometimes it sounds surreal. Sometimes it comes outside of myself. Sometimes it comes from other sides of myself. The voice in the journal does not fill out business reports, write columns or give speeches. It does not look to see if its shoes are tied or its clothes are on inside out. The voice in the journal has the heart of a child and the mind of an adult. In that way it may be more like myself. It may have changed over the time that I have been writing. I don't know.

—Becke Roughton

When my journal voice comes through in conversation, it's always shocking in its articulateness and clarity. In the journal it's a voice that's wide-ranging and various, but in conversation it only comes out when pressed to the wall, either defending myself or another, or trying to help someone out of a desperate sink, or spouting off descriptions and analyses of some desperate sink of my own. And yes, it has changed. Faster, looser, less sentimental. I turn to the journal when I want to whine and rage and complain, when something happens, when nothing happens, when the perceiving and arranging and order-making part of my mind is stuffed too full for the memory part to balance properly. I go to the journal when there are events (material and otherwise) to be recorded—when, in other words, I'm simply here. I write things down in the first place because that's the only way I really remember them.

I write in order to find out what's there. I keep a journal in order to have a collection of "things that are there" from which to choose. I write things down in order to make them real. In order to figure them out.

The journal's importance to me: Things are only half real if they haven't been sifted for meaning. For me, that means putting them down into words. In my journal I sometimes forget that language is a lie, or else I simply don't care.

—Brenda Murphree

I keep a journal to allay the fear of oblivion, and to keep records. I like to keep track of what happens to me, and to write because I am a writer instinctively. I teach writing, and I read writers. Life seems clearer and more enjoyable when I write down what I think. It is an active process, and really changes how I act and live. It helps me to believe in the life I am living.

—Jacklyn W. Potter

The journal lets me keep my life.
It keeps me sane. Because of course,
I can get my feelings out, thoughts,

I can analyze. It keeps me in touch
with myself, who I am, the changing,
ever changing I.

—Sally Sullivan

I can begin a writing session out of sorts, feeling sorry for myself and reach a place of relative peace in the process of writing it out. The diary is by nature lonely work. I feel alone, but not lonely, however. I welcome the solitude, the deliberate pulling away from the outside and letting the inward flow take over. The journal is an extension of me, or as Progoff puts it, the embodiment of a life in process. I can't imagine my life without it, but I don't consider it an addiction or a burden. It's necessary, like breathing.

—Elaine Goolsby

Writing in my journal has everything to do with composition of thought. I simply think better when I write out my thoughts. I am an intuitive thinker, and how blissfully happy I am when I am thinking intuitively. Out of necessity, perhaps, all these years, my journal has functioned simply as pages where I check and double-check the condition of my life and pages out of which solutions to problems emerge.

—Nancy Simpson

I write whenever I am deeply moved by something I didn't expect to happen. When I hurt, I write. When I am sad, I write. When I am happy, sometimes I will write. The older I get, the easier it is becoming for me to write down the things that are also good around me.

—Amy Wilson

Sometimes I feel that I live my life in these pages, as if my nose were pressed against the paper. It's hard to see the threads of development, for peering at the daily. I need perspective. Sometimes I wonder what the themes, what the thesis of what I have written are. Sometimes I think I would gain distance if it were typed. I would almost feel as if someone else had written it. Handwriting is so intimate. Everything seems to lose the essence of objectivity, sort of like reading a love letter.

I want to use the journal to do more than just spin my wheels. There are areas now where I can perhaps write and grow. I have read about people whose journal writing kept them going over the same ground. I feel as if I'm not really doing all I can with my journal. Some days I do, but other days I just skim.

—Agnes McDonald

I pushed myself to write about things I don't feel comfortable about. Mostly my own bad traits. It is galling in writing to have to admit in writing one's own undesirable thoughts and feelings, mean streaks.

I am struck by how negative my journal seems, the same problems, over and over. But I'm glad I work them out through writing.

—Gwynne Glover Hackworth

I keep a journal because I like to look at things on paper. I like looking backward and forward and here, now. I like seeing who I used to be and who I am now. I like to think that my son will read my journal someday and know better the person who is his mother. I see my journal as a means to understanding myself better, a record of what I see, like the red-bellied woodpecker this snowy morning, or feel, like the grief when my nephew died.

—Joy Averett

> **Whatever** I don't know
> what to do with goes here, my
> spewings and frothings at the
> mouth/mind. Other than that
> it helps me grow by delays
> or keeping growing through delays. I
> sure as hell don't try to be pretty or
> poetic in my journal. The old
> school voice is what I want to
> avoid in my journal unless it pops
> out full blown. I want to catch
> what comes because there lies the
> truth of me. I am a gut made manifest
> in my journal. Whatever beauty is in
> my soul will emerge.

—Nancy Markham

May 23, 1992—I realize that my journal is a combination of scribbled dream remnants and thoughts that surface the moment I awaken. Sometimes I cannot distinguish the difference between dream and morning. I wonder about the kind of person who writes in her journal at mid-day, or at the closing of the day, one with a satisfying relationship, or a troubled one, one who lives alone after years of being married, as I do, or one who has had only her cat for years.

I am not comfortable in "confession" groups. Always, I censor myself, even as I learned to do with my psychiatrist. Because I have always found judgment. Once, my therapist had to complete a form for me, for a job. In the boxes he had to check, he placed the "x" just a little closer to the right of the box, closer to the square that indicated "problem." Everything else was checked squarely in the middle of the boxes right down the line. I have never trusted him or anyone to judge me in a confidential manner since. This morning I feel the value of my journal, my friend. Everywhere else I feel like Narcissus, that my secret will spring from the earth. My journal I can shred or burn.

August 1–Periodically, I review my journal. Always I am surprised. My journal is my therapist, my private repository of my responses to my inner and outer world. Sometimes I am horrified by an outpouring of pain and anger, like the dumping of dirty scrub water flecked with bits of debris tracked in by family, friends and me. Sometimes I see a glimmer of hope and sunlight. Anyway, I am grateful for the gift of language with which to approximate my thoughts and feelings.

Today the floor shines, tribute to an hour of dip, squeeze, wipe. I wish that I did not have to continually, regularly clean the film of dirt, both from my floors and from my soul. I enjoy my daily showers. Cleansing the body gives me a lift, a fragrance and energy that I find pleasant.

I do not enjoy the effort to cleanse my feelings; my disgust with the stupidity of racism, sexism, violence, political ignorance and apathy, economic ineptness, the degradation of our home planet. All these are the sum total of fear. Study and experience reveal the reality of cycles throughout nature. My soul cleansing, no doubt, reflects nature's cycles. Nevertheless, it is wearing—the eternal theme and variation.

—Gwendoline Y. Fortune

PLACE

Know your place. Stay in your place. Your place is with me. Your place is in the home. As an indicator of rank and station, the word place has an unpleasant ring for women. We have worked hard not to hear it, not to heed it. And all the while, we have watched. We have soaked up scenes with our pores. For every window, there is a woman who has stared through it. Every detail of sight, sound and smell has been stamped on her cells. A fine line, literally, runs from her eyes, down her arm through her fingers, and onto the page. So, there is scarcely a page in southern journals that does not begin with a description, or at least a reference, to where the writer is. But life is more than a room with a view, particularly if the room is a kitchen.

We love the place names of the South, names like Silk Hope, Red Springs, Meadow and Collie Swamp. We say these names and we write them, and they taste mighty good on the tongue, hang around in the mouth and mind like fume from brandied figs, even if bad memories of these places make it hard to love the place itself. Kudzu grottoes in rain, doves in fresh cut grass, jasmine sweet and sticky in the air, perhaps even the Dallas airport, are interwoven with us. Sometimes we have to forget, sometimes revise the memory of farm or town, not so much how it looked, but how it was or how we thought it was. The meanest, picky little details cling to us like beggar's lice. They

7

get carried down that long lonesome road
before we notice they are there. The best instru-
ment to remove them is the pen.

Places on the verge of extinction have to
be preserved, or they will die with us. We may
swap versions and compare versions, but this is
only diversion. We keep our own accounts, dis-
tortions, errors and all.

Place is not only what we write about
and under the spell of, but where we write.
Snatching time for a cup of tea and a few pages
in our bedroom rocker, in a booth at Burger
King, in the dentist's office, in a car headed west
on the interstate, journal writers use some
places to shut out others.

Typically there is writing of inner
weather. The cliffs and valleys of the mind's
topography are mirrored in falling snow, rolling
hills, gusts of wind through pine trees, the fertile colors of crops. And when a woman makes
small sense of tragic news or the heart's confu-
sion, a walk through a church yard or familiar
scenes in the family album help to ground her.

Place can be an anchor or a millstone.
Uprooted, mobile (although our poorer sisters
have always known about that), the corporate or
academic, relocated woman is the uptown version of the migrant moving on to look for work.
And the instincts can be the same. Carry cut-
tings from another garden, light the fire and
lamps, hang curtains, lay quilts and write. The
journal too is place. Where the heart is, words
are not far behind.

WHERE? | Jo Jane Pitt

November 5, 1990

A couple of weeks ago—no, more like three or four, wonderful rain. I have always loved rain, still do. Yet it is a challenge to be wholly grateful for drought's end. This valiant little substandard house I have rented for over ten years succumbs—at least the living room and dining room ceilings do.

I am depressed as I set out pots, plastic bowls and large yogurt containers. I stand and wait for drips from the cracked plaster, long peeling.

Depressed because this house was a blessing when I found it; frustrated by the hopeless, helpless financial situation—lowish income single mom; repulsed by the ugliness of this little dwelling with its brown asbestos shingles, overgrown shrubs, warped roof, separating walls. The walls are filthy, peeling from them is the ten-year-old cheap paint slapped on by then husband, just out for the first time from an alcohol recovery center, and me, classic co-dependent. Every year, I thought was my last here. But I need three bedrooms, one for daughter and one for son. The other is my study, where I have bed and clothes closet. I am a writer. The neighborhood isn't scenic but safe and convenient.

I teach college freshman composition for a living. I am not significantly published and I do not have a Ph. D. I like my work; I have the best position of its kind in the area. Still, I work all the time and cannot adequately support a family.

Recovering single mom co-dependent, writer, teacher.

In baseball, that's called three strikes.

I try to turn over my worries to a higher power as the drips pop into plastic and alternately ping into metal.

But I do not really turn over this problem; actually I try to ignore it. I lie on the very ragged sofa under the red lap afghan and drive the remote through the channels to look for some program semi-mindless enough for background to get me through at least half a set of compositions. I have four sets, at least sixty-five essays. Each one needs individual attention.

I am maintaining a fairly balanced mental attitude for this period of not writing. I become unhealthy when I cannot write—at least journal for therapy. The creative absorption for the other—poetry, fiction, the unfinished screenplay—is on hold. For how long I do not know.

I am glad Eden is at school this weekend of the rain, Aaron at his dad's. Alone with plop-drip. Easier to push aside.

Ignore. Pray/plead.

I do not have any other option. At least not tonight.

November 9, 3:10 p.m.

Rain again. Predictions of frost. At last the air is to turn cold. A couple of weeks ago the ceiling leaks began. Indian summer nurtured my forgetfulness. Procrastination.

My mother called, distressed; her company cut back her hours. There goes her small part-time income, and more importantly, her sense of worth.

I scrounge for the pots and plastic containers to put them under the drips. The cracks meander across the plaster. The large picnic basket and metal album rack stuffed with old albums tucked behind the end table are dangerously close to the drip in the living room ceiling's front corner and edge. If I slide them down behind the soda, they will be closer to the heat vent. I move them across the room to add to the clutter in the corner by the encyclopedia book shelf. In front of the unused extra door to Eden's room.

I don't know why I think of the plants on the old TV cart on the front porch. I begin to bring in the plants. New drips begin in the kitchen. The main problem there is they are soaking the extension cord into which are plugged blender, coffee maker, toaster. I remember something about water, electricity, shock and fire. Danger.

The plop and ping of the drips in all the metal and plastic in the three rooms are the particular trigger of my depression.

Four more drips in a row almost in the center of the dining room ceiling are new with this rainfall.

I lift and loop the tangle of cords over the little shelf under the kitchen window and wipe them dry with a dish towel, after the slightest hesitation about that water and electricity and shock stuff. This doesn't feel like the moment and place for my death.

But does it ever?

There is the exact moment—when I am lying on the couch listening to the pings and plops before I bring in the plants, or after I have offered them to their indoor showers, and after the phone call from Eden, and I am again lying on my sofa seeking some serenity from meditation, invoking my guardian angels and guides, even as my thoughts are racing and my adrenalin is spiraling like crazy—there is an exact moment (to remind you of the point of the meander) when I confront—when truth and fact and reality and illusion, delusion and vision converge.

I have got to move.

Out of this house.

As soon as possible.

Stuck here for ten years. Every year hoping to get out.

Finally, this year with Eden out of college in May and Aaron out of high school next year, I decide—pray—okay, I've been here this long. Just let me get the kid out of high school; then I'll figure out what next.

I still love you, rain, I do. But this is hard.

Eden calls as I am watching for drips from living room corner.

She says, "Oh, Mom, I'm sick and bummed. I'm burned out. Tired of school." This from the professional student who pines for school after a two-week break. She says, "I want my Mommy." She has not been home for over a month. I have missed her and we unload. We remark that we are usually depressed at the same time. I tell her about Grannie's job, about putting plants under drips, and four sets of papers to catch up on. I tell her I am talking on the new cordless phone she hasn't seen. I finally invested; leasing phones is renting. I just never had the money all at one time to buy. I am very careful with credit cards.

I lie on the couch and "veg" with the TV. It is settled. I am moving out of this house. Soon. I don't have the slightest idea how. Or where.

I remember.

When I was little, after Daddy died, my mother always said if she couldn't work, "they" would put our furniture out on the street, and we wouldn't have a roof over our heads.

RED SUN EMERGING | Susan Broili

November 10, 1990, 8:30 a.m., Forty-nine degrees

Chilly rain, so hard it sounded like a thousand cat feet ripping across the roof, sent me into dreams of tranquil waters, clear and blue, in places like Tortola, St. Thomas, and Virgin Gorda, where shallow pools offer "excellent snorkeling" according to guide books.

Actually, this drifting is moored in reality: the free airline ticket to the Caribbean, given to me by my sister on my birthday last month— the trip we're planning for January. What I should be doing is dreaming up the money to pay for the rest of the trip, for we are going where the rich winter. Rag-tag birds like us usually fly over these islands in search of low-rent perches.

Judy provides the answer in the way she went about going to Russia. She made her dream happen. Making dreams happen begins and ends in the imagination. First, the dream—something longed for— what your psyche requires to flower. Too many of us play it safe—some to the point of refusing to dream at all—or if we do, to feel guilty about indulging in such fantasies. Too many of us go through life like a tight bud, which never opens to the sun. We do not flower to brighten the world and fill the air with our scent: attract hummingbirds, butterflies, and bees.

I dream of attracting publishers—and readers. If I am going to realize my dream, I have to spend more time writing. Next week, I'm

going to get up earlier—at six a.m.—so I can have two hours to write
before getting ready to go to work.

November 20, 6:50 a.m., Forty-seven degrees
There is not much color in the world yet. It's dark and gray. I
hear a jet overhead, the swish of a car on the street beyond the patio, the
hum of a heat pump (not mine). Saving money for the Caribbean trip, I
sit here with a coat on, a blue scarf around my neck and a full cup of
steaming coffee at my side.
Even as I write, the day gets brighter—gray mackerel clouds,
dappled in peach, as if painted by a French impressionist. The background blue is getting bluer by the minute. The sun has crested the tops
of the pines, while the clouds above gleam as if cast in gold.
The sun also rises on St. Thomas, its back to the cold Atlantic, its
face turned toward the warm, clear turquoise Caribbean. There are no
pine trees to block the sun. I imagine a molten red ball rising from the
sea, signaling flocks of hummingbirds that it is time to seek the nectar,
time for the acacia, bougainvillea and frangipani to bloom and fill the air
with their scent. If I close my eyes, I can almost smell the sea, hear it lap
the sugar sand, feel the tropical sun warm me to the bone—even my
toes, now encased in socks.

November 27, 10:23 p.m., Sixty degrees
Last night, I hardly slept at all. At least not the deep sleep which
rests body and soul. The cause of this anxiety was THE LIST—posted yesterday at work. THE LIST of new assignments in the new, merged newspaper come January first. THE LIST in which more hopes were dashed
than raised. The sportswriter, who wanted to work in the Life section, saw
his hope die when he was listed as sports copy editor. "I'll be a clerk," he
told me. The woman who enjoyed working on the medical beat saw, to
her great surprise, Chapel Hill Herald writer beside her name. In one
stroke, she had been replaced. And the man who thought he had made it
clear he would not like to work only nights, metro night editor.
THE LIST goes on.
At first glance, I thought the designation beside my name meant
I would be writing and editing the entertainment magazine, just like
before—until I mentioned this to the man who would be editor of the
Life section. He indicated he had other ideas—the first such indication.
"Let's talk," he said.
We have much to talk about. I have been going over points I
want to make. Dialogue is important—essential to communication. Up-
front communication is essential to building trust. Trust is essential to a
good relationship—business or otherwise. When maneuvers are made
behind a person's back and then abruptly brought to a person's attention,
then distrust follows.

Sentence without trial. Totalitarian rule. Authoritarian. The plantation system, in which human beings are seen only as work-producing units, mules, and so, as Toni Morrison so movingly writes in Beloved, are listed on the animal side of the ledger page.

THE LIST.

January 1, 1991, 10:00 a.m., Thirty-six degrees

What a way to begin the new year: listening to Bach's Brandenburg Concertos, watching the house finches feed on the patio, smelling the paperwhites.

My New Year. I sit here ready to begin—a cup of hot coffee to my right. A warm cat, Big Kitty, snuggled against my left side. I face the New Year with a sense of joy, expectation, adventure and a touch of sadness and loss. Sadness because yesterday was the last day of *The Durham Sun*, a spirited newspaper for almost a hundred and two years. A victim—not of television—but of corporate mentality which looks to the ledger sheet and doesn't listen to the heart of the community. The *Sun*'s editor looked so sad. I was afraid to say too much to him because I feared we'd both start sobbing. I am allowing the tears now that I denied yesterday. A good cry for what was and will never be again. Instead of merger, it was murder. Death of *The Durham Sun*.

My long time as entertainment editor, nine years—eight for The Sun and one as editor for a merged section prior to the merger of both papers—has come to an end—at my request, in view of the circumstances. I did not want the work and worry without clear decision-making authority. My new schedule as a staff writer will give me more time in the mornings to do my own writing at home—writing from the heart, not bound by time or place—as Ezra Pound once put it, "the news that stays news."

I am starting a new professional and personal life, and I know I can let go of the other, shed it like a dried-out skin, slip out of it and glide through the grass in search of a sunnier spot—such as the Caribbean. We leave January 22.

January 19, 7:30 a.m., Thirty-eight degrees

We are at war. We are without airline tickets to the Caribbean. The war started on Wednesday, when our planes bombed Baghdad. Today's headlines read: Missiles hit Israel again despite U. S. air efforts. And, at the top of the front page, above the masthead: Eastern Airlines bankrupt, scratches all flights.

When I heard the news flash last night, I was stunned, could think of nothing else. Even the war was brushed aside as I focused on the possibility that we would not go to the Caribbean. Dreams withered. Dreams revived again, however, after I talked to Jo last night. She had heard on CNN that American Airlines would honor Eastern vouchers—so she is going to the travel agent today to get us on an American flight.

Being concerned about taking this trip might seem trivial in the face of war, but it is important in the war of the spirit. My spirit has been under siege for some time now. It's squeezed together tight, like an accordion packed away, and needs to stretch out in one long, glorious, expansive note, waltz with gliding steps on the veranda overlooking St. Thomas harbor, with twinkling lights of cruise ships instead of the blinding flashes of cruise missiles.

February 22, 12:25 p.m., Seventy-one degrees, Cane Garden Bay, Tortola, British Virgin Islands

This is the most beautiful place I have ever seen. Arrived here at noon yesterday, after spending the night on St. Thomas, a busy place with much traffic, many shops and many cruise-ship shoppers. Our hotel, the Galleon House, was perched on the mountainside right in the heart of Charlotte Amalie. To get there, we climbed up and down several flights of steps past the Fiddle Leaf, an expensive French restaurant, past flaming Chinese hibiscus, Frangipani Temple Tree, pale, pink flowers with rose centers, which smelled sweet as coconuts. Past a giant yucca, where lizards skittered over the broad, flesh leaves. Past fiery crepe paper bougainvillea. Past towering palms, fronds rustling in the easterly breeze. To the Galleon House veranda to check in. Then a cold drink and a sit on the veranda, where we could see the harbor—too beautiful to be real—filled with huge cruise ships, sailboats of all sizes—anchored in brilliant turquoise water as if an artist had held back nothing, filled the canvas with the richest of colors. And, behind us, the pink-tiled houses stacked on the mountainside, with long flights of steps connecting perches along the steep slope.

The next day, bound for Tortola, our ferry, The Native Son, turned into a huge speedboat, which slapped waves, sending up whale-sized plumes. About halfway into the forty-five minute ride, a cabin boy, walking with sea-legged surety, appeared, carrying a tray of cups brim-ful of liquid red as hummingbird food, which he served to passengers. I drank several gulps of the sweet, fruit-tasting liquid before he reap-peared, this time with a bottle of rum, which he dribbled into any want-ing cup.

On the way, we passed small, muffin-shaped islands. We sped by St. John's Caneel Bay, Hawksnest Bay, Trunk Bay (one of the most beautiful beaches in the world) and on to Tortola. Upon disembarking, we lined up at a visitor's sign to go through customs. Another line took care of residents and belongers (natives). On a form, we had to check reason for being there: business or pleasure, and I gleefully checked pleasure. On to a taxi van, which we shared with a couple from Pennsyl-vania, who were going to The Moorings to pick up a thirty-four-foot ketch and would then sail around the islands for who knows how long. On the way to The Moorings, right outside of Road Town, we passed several baby goats trotting along together. No mother in sight.

February 25, 7 a.m., Upper seventies, Cane Garden Bay, Tortola, British Virgin Islands
Jo and I slept in yesterday—after a late night of dancing to a band called Trouble at the Paradise Beach Bar and later to a reggae-calypso band, Blue Haze, at another beach bar called The Wedding. I danced the night away with C. (a major experience, much too much to go into right now).

Still, by noon, we had our backpacks on and were headed along the road leading out of Cane Garden Bay. We passed baby goats, the ubiquitous chickens. We stopped to smell the gardenias, see the poinsettias, as we headed up—way up—stopping often to rest and enjoy the panoramic view of the bay, dotted with sailing yachts. Near the top of the ridge, we caught a ride and were soon jolting along the corkscrew road leading down to Brewers Bay.

Equipped with mask, snorkel and our underwater cameras, we set off for a self-guided tour of the bay. Gliding face-down, over patches of coral, I saw little blue, green and yellow fish and pale blue fish (blue tangs) and larger yellow fish with silvery sides, feeding on the live coral: fans, brain and tubular orange clusters. It was hypnotic—moving through schools of neon-striped fry, getting very close to other fish, which seemed to have no fear of me. It was hard to come out of the water, but, finally, due to the pain from my face mask cutting into my forehead, I reluctantly returned to shore. Jo and I shared a peanut butter-and-jelly sandwich, Cheetos and a diet Coke as we contemplated paradise: an unspoiled beach, bordered by jungle and thirty-foot coconut palms, on a wide bay in which no yachts were moored. We watched pelicans dive for fish. We hunted for shells—very exotic-looking shells, unlike any found on North Carolina beaches. Again, I got that I-could-stay-here-forever feeling. We leave tomorrow—on Tuesday.

March 3, 7:45 a.m., Fifty-five degrees
Cool and gray. Overcast. No sun. This time, in Tortola, the clouds are rubbing the stony backs of the mountains. The sun is already warm. The frigates soar, spreading their three-foot wings to catch air currents. The pelicans dive for a breakfast of fry. I am still caught in the spell of Tortola. I feel as if I am more there than here. Oh, I hear the pingpoints of rain on the chimney flue, see the thin curtain of gray fall to the ground, hear the mournful call of the dove, which echoes my own sadness at having to leave Tortola. It is such a beautiful place, with its half-moon bays. The sea has sculpted a gentle curve into the land, like the curve of arms which hold a lover, cradle a child, like the curve of the

womb, safe and secure. I have never seen the world from this bay view—the unbroken circle of sky and sea, rimmed with land, a cosmos easily grasped. The sight of it made me gasp at the sheer beauty. At night, the stars added their magic.

Though our days—and nights—were busy in Tortola, I felt a deep sense of peace. No stress. I felt it leave me the minute I looked out on Cane Garden Bay. The gentle curve of the bay swings the hips of the land into a dance with the sea and sky. The wind blows a musical beat, rattling coconut palms like giant maracas, while pelican splashes rumba the water.

This dance from the hips. This Caribbean song. If the hips are supple, if the hips swing uninhibited, the rest of the body is free to follow. But first, you must hear the music, feel it in your body. I must remember this song, this dance, for I have been too afraid to move to it, to give myself up to this rhythm of life.

March 7, 2:15 p.m., Hot, hot, hot, Brewers Bay Campground, Tortola, British Virgin Islands

From my seat under the tent awning, I can see turquoise water in jigsaw-puzzle patterns through fronds of young coconut palms. Very breezy and cool under here, very hot on the bay. It was hot, hot, hot last night in more ways than one.

I had decided I was going to Cane Garden Bay to hear Quito Rymer play at his beach bar, Quito's Gazebo, where Jo and I had gone last year. Packed my backpack with camera, other necessities, including a bottle of water. I put on my walking shoes. If I couldn't catch a ride, I'd have to hike up the torturous, steep, hairpin turns leading out of Brewers Bay. No ride. Huffed and puffed my way up. At one rest stop, I heard the welcomed sound of a car engine eating road. Got a ride all the way to the top where the driver lived.

Walk down to Cane Garden Bay, long, steep, hard on knees, which threatened to lock. Then, on the other side of the road, I saw a Tortolan, wearing baggy, African-inspired pants, like MC Hammer wears. He was jogging backwards down the mountain. I tried it, only I walked instead of jogged. Much better on the knees. When I heard a car coming, I'd turn around and walk forward. Slowly, I made my way backwards and forwards down the steep slope. Goats scampered across the road as I turned the final curve and walked down into the village of Cane Garden Bay. I stopped to watch the sunset turn clouds into buttermilk ripples as the hot yolk of sun sizzled into the sea. Silhouetted against the silken sea and sky were sailing yachts and fishermen, standing up in their small boats as they pulled in their nets.

By this time, I had really worked up an appetite for Quito's barbecue dinner. Spotted a couple from Idaho, who were staying at the campground, and joined them at their table on the balcony. While we were eating, I saw the back of a man tying his dinghy up on one of the balcony posts. He was wearing a straw hat and a white, sleeveless T-shirt. Could it be C., the man I had met and danced with last year—the one who almost seduced me? (Only fear of getting AIDS had brought me to my senses. This time, I had brought protection.) The next time I turned to look, the man was seated at the farthest bar stool. His face was in shadow. From what I could see, he didn't look like C. I turned back around. Idaho couple left after listening to Quito play a few songs.

It wasn't long before I saw the man with straw hat out on the dance floor. It was C. He was dancing with this woman. My heart sank. He was here with someone. About this time, a man from Dominica asked me to dance.

"You're a good dancer," he said. So was he. We danced several dances. Then, I spotted Shadow at the bar and went over and said hello. He owns a horse farm high above Brewers Bay and makes a living taking tourists on horseback rides. Jo and I had gone riding with him last year.

"Last year, you were nervous. This year, you're a regular home-girl," said Shadow, who had been watching me dance.

Somewhere in all this dancing, I caught C.'s eye and said hello. As I sat down, with the Dominica man not far behind, C. passed by and said, "Save me a dance," the same thing he had said last year. A little later, as I was headed back to my table, he walked up and, in a firm voice, said, "I want to talk to you—over there," as he nodded toward the far end of the balcony bar.

And there, as we sat face to face, I told him that one reason why I wanted to see him again was to thank him.

"I had not allowed men in my life for a long time. You changed that."

Then, we danced. What a good dancer. I had had an opportunity to watch him dance earlier. He had an in-command, sensual way of moving—from the hips—an easy, exotic grace. We danced and danced and before I knew it, Quito was singing his last song: Bob Marley's "Could You Be Loved?"

Earlier, C. had said he could give me a ride in his dinghy back to Brewers Bay. His fifty-foot ship, with eight passengers aboard, was moored in Cane Garden Bay. They had been too tired to come in to hear the music. "First night," said C., who would spend the next week sailing them around the islands—how he made his living.

"What was THAT?" I said, as a big, silver form leaped out of the water just a few feet from our boat.

"Gar. Sharp teeth," said C., who had his hands full watching out for fish traps.

"Could a gar land in the boat?"

C. nodded, "Yes."

At the mouth of Brewers Bay, he located the channel—safe passage through waters full of reefs.

Once ashore, I located the path leading from the beach to my tent and led the way up the narrow trail laddered with roots and canopied with young coconut palms.

"Do you do this often?" said C., sounding a little apprehensive, which made me feel a bit like a bewitching Calypso leading Odysseus to her cave.

"No," I said, thinking never, never have I done this—surprising myself at my boldness. Later, I sat in a chair on the beach near my path and watched the bright star of his flashlight until it disappeared around the point.

And I wished for his safe return to his ship.

May you skirt the reefs, the fish traps. May the gar stay out of your boat. And, may I see you again some Caribbean night.

I had one more day on this beautiful bay—then, I had to leave this island—again.

March 23, 9:30 p.m., Forty-five degrees

Listening to Vladimir Horowitz play the piano—his first performance in Moscow after years of exile—the sad, haunting quality of the music—and I was overcome, put my hand to my forehead, closed my eyes, so intense the emotions, so overwhelmed was I by the memory of meeting C. again, quite by chance, on my second trip, last month, to the Caribbean, when I seized the moment, going for an intense connection with another person after so many years of hesitations, lost chances. My pen races now as fast as the music, skipping, tremoloing along. No matter what happens, I am glad I did it.

Any life fully lived fills with poignancy, that deep catch in the throat, yearning for what once was and can never be again, yearning for what never was: hopes, dreams never realized.

My horoscope today: "Set your sights on a specific objective and go after it. Although other people may call you a dreamer, you can succeed."

And his: "Be flexible in your closest relationships. You need to give a little, especially when it comes to affairs of the heart."

Who, if anyone, is C. romancing now? The price of caring can be heartache. Don't place so much importance on this one man, I tell myself. Don't care for him too much. He is far away in another world, from another world. Maybe he didn't care at all. Maybe he cared a lot. Maybe he still does. Sometimes chance meetings can transcend barriers, hold worlds, retain a hold on the heart.

In many ways, Tortola seems like home, where my spirit unfolds, blossoms. There the colors fill all the way to my outer lines, a once-blank coloring book, now saturated with vibrant hues as red as the hibiscus, as blue, green and yellow as the parrot fish.

April 15, 7:00 a.m., Fifty-three degrees

Cloudy with a lake of pale gold. Somewhere, just below this lake, behind the tops of pines, the sun tries to erupt, burn through the clouds. The sun is my spirit attempting to shine through all the doubts, obstacles to what I want to be: a woman who loves and is loved, a woman who loves herself, believes in herself, who accomplishes what she sets out to do.

I want to write that novel about a woman's transformation. I want to write a detective series in which the heroine is a travel writer, which will put her (and me, because I'll have to do the research) in all sorts of exotic locations. I want to write poetry and journal—and publish all these different forms.

Now, the molten ball of fire burns above the pines, turning the sky into a lake of liquid gold. Its magic alchemy gilds the fuzzy stems of the scented geranium on my writing table. The sun turns my eyelashes into a fringe of iridescent rainbows. The sun dapples me with light. Its warmth flows over me and through me. I am a child of light, born on a Sunday, a sunny day. I seek light the way the Antillean-crested hummingbird is drawn to the golden blooms of the century plant, which grows in the Caribbean.

I grow in the Caribbean. There, my spirit expands. There, I am a sponge, soaking up the atmosphere, letting the water flow in and out, siphoning the details. I can feel my edges, but at the center, there's a sense of infinite joining.

I merge with the crystalline sea. I am the purple sea fan, waving in the tidal flow and the angel fish which nibbles the fan. I am the trade winds and the black frigate bird, which rides the wind. I am the coconut palm, which rattles its fronds, bends to the wind, and so does not break—even in hurricanes.

I am the almond tree. I shake my fruit and the green pods covering the sweet nut pelt the sand, like raindrops thrown down by Zeus.

I am the scorpion, the snake, the ghost crab, the lizard, looking at life through hooded eyes, which peel away all scales of illusion, seeing through and into everything.

I am the red sun emerging from the turquoise sea. I shake off steaming, salty drops, a blue tang fish or two, and rise, changing the gray sky into the diaphanous, silk canopy of saffron and tangerine.

WHERE COLD WATERS RUN FINE | Brenda Murphree

July 13

Way off in the mountains, where the cold waters run fine and clear as a spilling wine, there is a small piece of land. It belongs to no one in particular; it is marked as a "small piece of land" by the absence of ownership, or, more precisely, by the lines of already owned land which surround it.

On the small piece of land is a small meadow where creeping charlies lazily sprawl, and four-o'clocks and primroses occasionally peek out from the yellow-tasseled field grasses. And there are tall croppings of southern pines, almost everywhere, and the hills breathe noticeable, slight rippling heaves, as if to remind themselves that yes, all is still here, all is still the same, every day as dusk slides into the valleys.

The valleys themselves lie like enormous laps, or cradles, creaking, tired, forgotten. After years of neglect, years of holding no one to rock, they still coo gently, absently, through the first long hours of night as if to say, "There now, you will wake again tomorrow, and tomorrow after that, and it will all be the same."

And the hills breathe softly, and the pines murmur in sleep. And the waters run on like a clear wine spilling down the grass-matted lap of a giant queen.

Here I sit in my quiet blue and green two-story home with Baroque music lilting forth and the kettle humming and money (relatively speaking) and am still missing that land of "the lowly and invincible of the earth, who endure and endure and endure—tomorrow and tomorrow and tomorrow."

But this I love too. Gale winds here now (and all afternoon). Tornado warnings. This afternoon one of the plants at the front window was knocked over with its stand, dirt dumped all over the carpet. Hurricanes I understand, but this only makes me nervous. Music, incense, tea, even the mindless winds—this is my world. I have my feet in more than one.

A PROSPECT OF APPLES | Lynn Powell

February 12, 1983

Most incredible snowfall yesterday. We only measured nineteen inches, but I'd wager there's near two feet. Certainly more in drifts. Dan and I skied down to the White Hall General Store and saw our first purple finch—"like a sparrow dipped in raspberry juice," or as Dan asked, "Is that really its color or did someone spray paint it?"

Only human-made things looked waylaid, wading up to their waists in snow. The trees, weeds, fountain-like bushes, all looked proportional, just scaled down by the snow at their feet.

Met the Methodist minister and the store owner who's been in the grocery business "for years, all over." "Where?" "Crozet, Standardsville, Ivy . . ."

Skied back home through sunset which meant, with the sky all smoke, the snow had all the light. The wind had kept the snow out of trees, hedges, weeds migrating through the fields, so there were streaks of deep evergreen and lines of gold, luminous in the slow evaporation of light.

This morning the birds came to the seeds we threw out yesterday: juncos and one song sparrow.

April 23

On Wednesday went to Frances B.'s house to deliver information about the march. Frances: a wee woman with her rumpled tuft of white hair, wearing the deepest purple from her shoes to her wide, tasseled scarf tied in a band about her head. A warbling little voice that teeters on an edge but never falls.

I had imagined Frances' house to be like any grandma's house. But as I entered it, I noticed how unkept the shrubs and yard. The two junipers beside the walk, before the porch, had grown to unruly heights; they completely blocked the porch. Then, the foreshadowing clutter. I laughed when I saw a green CARTER/MONDALE 1976 bumper sticker held within the decorative metal of the screen door.

Inside, though, I caught my breath. It was dark, and a tangle of trinket, artifact, junk, art covered every surface—horizontal and vertical. I was spooked, awestruck. I had entered art—a movie or a story— Faulkner or Cervantes I couldn't yet tell. This woman had the singularity, suddenly, of a character.

"I paint everything that doesn't move," she warbled. And that seemed true: the ceilings, the light switches, the precious space among the avalanche of objects. She painted flowers, mostly, in those bright, unqualified, shiny colors the Mexicans use.

Hers was the least discriminating, most acquisitive taste/imagination I have ever encountered. On the living room table, I guess you'd call it—Lord knows where she found the space to set her plate and glass—was this season's decoration: a large carved Christ on the cross presiding over trays of Easter eggs (beautiful variegated stone eggs, Ukrainian painted ones, cheap plastic ones—all jumbled together), balloons knotted into crosses of four, plastic grass.

She cleared a mound of newspaper clippings from a chair for me to be able to sit down. She said she had traveled all over the world— China, Africa, Russia, Mexico (where she had lived four years), Europe.

Everywhere she had, it was obvious, collected the folk art, the symbols (transient or permanent) of the people: a Nazi flag curtained the library's glass door.

She sent me upstairs alone for a tour—"Be sure to look at my pillow and see if you know what it is . . ." The barrage was relentless— mannequins at the top of the stairs gestured in their deepest purple clothes. In a room off to the left, a bed was piled with hats—mostly out-dated, purple contraptions with netting or outlandish flowers. There were a few mannequin heads among the clutter. Across the hall was her bedroom, cushioned in purple. A photograph (sepia) of her as a bride in the twenties on her dresser; a framed, yellowed certificate for her work with German Youth (my heart raced till I saw 1953). I turned to look at her pillow; there was a carved skeleton about fifteen inches long, its legs crossed, lolling on the pillow, with a deep purple, doll-sized, velvet hat with flowers on its skull! Faulkner, it was! How could I say to her I'd seen it? I looked beneath the skeleton and saw Shalom cross-stitched on the pillow.

"Do you know what it was?" she warbled. "Yes . . . uh, Shalom . . . it means peace . . ." "No, no, the skeleton!" Oh, yes, I'd noticed the skeleton. Well, she said, it was hand-carved in Mexico. Bought by her during their equivalent of Halloween—a festival of bones, it sounded, when even their bread was molded to look like vertebrae or femurs. She keeps it on her pillow to remind her that soon she, too, will look like that. "It's the first thing I see every morning, and I then laugh 'Ah ha! I don't look like you yet! I have another day to live and to do as I wish!'"

There's more to tell—the three new galleries out back, their wil-lowy murals she paints from a scaffold, their conglomerate of images: Thomas Jefferson in a forest of trees budding, blooming, and bare through the four seasons . . .

May 24, Harlan, Kentucky

Felt good to weed a patch of flower garden in the sun and walk a couple of miles 'round Sunny Acres with Nannie after dinner. Earlier in the day we went to return dishes to friends who had brought food for the family on Thursday and Friday. One stop was to see a Mrs. Carr, eighty-seven years old. She met us at the door of her humble house "in the bottom by the branch." She was in a wheelchair, wearing the perfect great-grandmother dress: black cotton with little yellow flowers, a rounded collar, buttons to the neck, a belt covered in the cotton. Black great-grandmother shoes and the thick brown hose that make legs look nearly artificial. Her face was clear and rosy, soft-looking; her smile childlike and ready; her silver hair braided into a thick ribbon wound about her head. Though it was a beautiful day outdoors, it was a bit cool, and she'd built a fire in her furnace (next to the couch). We left the spring and sat down in summer. A simple woman, with the griefs and joys of a simple life. She nearly wept when she told of Martha Lee Goshen just like that losing her mind three weeks back. Neighbors all these years, and she was such a good Christian woman, nice to everybody. The hot, blowing furnace; the cheap, yellowed linoleum; the spare decorations, years old now—the cheap sort of romantic frivolity so beautiful to those stranded in the backwoods, I guess. For example, two glass bubble frames, a "plantation" painted on the background, and the silhouettes of a hoop-skirted belle with parasol and her beau painted on the bubble (superimposed on the scene like a third dimension).

Visiting Mrs. J. proved what the impulse for something "pretty" in these backwoods could lead to, when met with millions of dollars and a Barbara Cartland sensibility. A sickly green living room and baby grand piano painted the same green; a green chandelier-patterned, fuzzy wallpaper; deep pink velvet chairs and sofas; kelly green velvet loveseat and chairs; pink and green figurines—Japanese samurai and Southern hoop-skirted ladies. Lamps—each another version of pink or green— and each with a ring of large dangles, glass cut (cylinder and knob) into penises. Cheap gilt tables, vases. And the book spilled at my feet: a picture book about Princess Grace, one of Princess Di and Little William, one of the royal wedding.

I felt so much happier with Mrs. Carr, whose aspirations seemed more local, more tied to the prospect of apples from the heavy-bloomed trees beyond the porch.

PINES WITH SNOW FALLING   Sally Sullivan

November 11

Coffee is good—it's Eight O'clock, the stuff I used to get at A&P. Wilson's carries it. It was quite a surprise to find it there.

Very strange-looking outside—partly sunny with stormy clouds, and it's rained a little with very heavy wind gusts. It reminds me of a painting called "December Twilight" by—I can't remember. American artist; it'll come to me—Wyeth—Andrew Wyeth, I think. I'm not sure that the title is right either, but there's a very eerie light in the painting, and it's as if there's a storm somewhere away from the scene.

I love stormy days; I remember how I loved them growing up and I would love to snuggle in bed reading a book, occasionally looking out the window at the trees blowing. Sometimes I would lie on Mother's bed because it was so high, and she also had double-windows to the side. So I would lie across it and stare out at the pines swaying like gargantuan ballerinas, their arms overhead as they bent at their supple waists over and over. Then I would read after I'd stared for a long time.

Sometimes I would bring a book there so that I could stop periodically to gaze some more, if the storm got particularly virulent. And the smell after the rain of those piney woods was so nice, a rich, earthy smell from the damp earth together with the odor of pine needles and wet pine bark and sap.

I had some dreams last night that I should write down in my dream journal. I've been awake an hour, up for fifty minutes and all I've done is make coffee and write, and stare out the window.

December 2

I was thinking about Christmases in the woods behind Daddy's hospital. About the pines with snow falling so that they looked like a silkscreen; the snow sometimes in fat, moist flakes, others in thin dry powdery ones. But mostly I remember we had wet snow. And stepping on it made a wonderful wet crunch; it packed immediately. Then, in the morning, it'd have a thin icy crust on it and the crunch would be crisp and crackly. From inside the house, you could hear the crunch of footsteps through it. But not when it first fell, so wet and blank as forgetfulness. And then, I remember the living room on Christmas morning when we went in and the things from Santa were all tastefully displayed. Mother was really good at that. I remember especially the Christmas I got the tank, a model of a U. S. W. W. II job that climbed over all obstacles—pillows, other toys. It seemed a miracle to me—how did it do that, looking like a caterpillar with suction legs? And how cold it was—you could see your breath until the fire in the fireplace began to warm things up.

SALTINESS MIXED WITH BLUE | Lu Ellen Huntley-Johnston

June 4, 1986

Wednesday has wind with her and carries the message—be near, be nearly maybe, near your own water, not too close right now, but near like the beach is near, near enough—can I bear not to hear? This wind says roll and tumble, stretch dreams across lines, inside out and through and through, the truth of the matter is that the longer the longer the longer the better, hide out, hide in, hold up, wait and see when you can do the doing of it, the meaning of it, reality, vitality, my emotional mentality—too soon to tell if I will or won't be near—thinking, thinking, thinking of the times in between the times—last Saturday at the beach I watched you watch, you watched me watch you watch and later we showered sand off and made our way to another sea, you and me being in season—ah now look at this—I'm going again, off in the bluer dark, eyes closed and seeing what the moth is blinded by, light source of my own kind of woman, the woman I have become does desire something beyond mentioning the man—the man—where? Near enough—distant now, distrusting now? Honor the distance now and go beyond all the past.

February 25
Today winter comes back, just for show more than for any real reason. I woke up to the sound of wind blowing on the water and had drifted to sleep to the sound of winter rain. I know that the seasons are changing, and I realize that this is an in-between day. It's cold because the wind is blowing and not as cold as it could be, because the sun is breaking through. I am glad to see and feel the sun although the last days of gray have been a comfort, a soft blanket. I have wanted to be covered with warm, soft blankets. I have desired the soft, dreamy places inside my own house. I have not desired the company of many friends. But this day makes me want to renew my search that I had become lost in. I feel more of an old me, a good old me, a me that wants to howl with laughs, a me that wants to dare to shuffle, strut, or dance like a wild somebody, my body feels so just so . . . just so really alive and hungry and ready to run and tumble in ocean and clap up waves. I feel the sun on my face making my skin tight . . . smile a cry. Love me back.

February 26
I saw five ducks on the water this morning. Everything was morning. I think I had a dream last night about being at a large gathering around a large table, and people were being served according to where they were seated around the table. I got tired of waiting, so I left. Outside there were others waiting to get in to eat, but these were commoner folks. So I must have been in between—the tail end of one group and license to move freely among the others. "Be fresh." Invent today. Make it new. How about leaving here just long enough to go get a whiff of ocean? Or bring the ocean here? Or just wait and see what is on its way now. Assemble the morning, the smell of bacon left in the house, coffee and chicory, the sun out back on the water—shine today.

Mid-July
I somehow get a feeling that maybe today will be an answer to days on end and edge. Morning runs make a difference. Peaches and cantaloupe go well together. I may have a second cup of coffee and contemplate a swim. I tried to come to terms last night with intervals, and decided that all is well. I heard an owl early this morning. My favorite time of day is just before the sun comes up; here especially is a place to appreciate sounds. It's constant hum and splash and wing and chant. This morning's run gave a feeling of summer camp after a rain. Some

home this is, always calm and quiet and water. The tulip tree reminds me that in a dream I visited here first. And that weekend in April, my first night. I knew then a pattern of intervals. Finding each other again will happen and by then we'll know new branches and have seen reminders, like green moments. In front I choose to see autumn mountains and fires. The smell that makes me know it is your green and black jacket . . .

HEART WITH HOPES OF HARVEST   Joy Averett

January 12, 1982
>   Memories of kitchens
> the cabinet, white with drawers and a glass front that dishes were
> behind—I pulled down on Ven
> the tiny mouse on the cabinet—I said "boo" to it and ran.
> my Grandmother Babcock's kitchen
>   the warmer over the stove
>   the margarine I squeezed the coloring right into
>   and the taste of the margarine with chewing gum
> my Grandmother Burwell's warmer over the stove (cold biscuits
>   or cornbread?)
> Aunt Maggie's benches and long table and little room with bed
>   right off her bedroom
>   Backyards from my childhood
> sitting with Uncle Buck under the locust tree
> Ven's falling out of the window into the backyard
> looking at star-shaped leaves of sweet gum tree
> the "hill" that seemed so steep when my legs were short
> learning to count to 100 while walking to the garden with Nat
>   (carrying a bucket of butter beans)
> the pear tree in Grandmother's back yard
>   pulling off my fingernail with the BB gun
> finding arrowheads in the field behind the mule, the plow, Daddy
> the long rain that we ran to watch
> the mean rooster in Mrs. Hughes' yard near the packhouse
> the bees in the back of the kitchen wall
> the swing on the tree on the little hill where I broke my arm
>   sliding on ice
> the mulberry trees and purple mouths

July 22

Daddy came for Sunday dinner—tomatoes, biscuits, squash cooked with onion, snaps (well-done), baked chicken, mashed potatoes, zucchini, eggplant, onions, and tomatoes—cold iced tea, coffee, blueberry pie (blueberries picked from our bushes and my very best pastry!). As we were eating the pie, Daddy said, "Some people have so much to eat, and some people don't have anything."

I often feel that way too, and it makes me want to choke on all this food we stuff into our bodies, swelling our skin until we look bumpy and grotesque. Daddy told us about tricking Charlie Wilson into eating a hot green one while he ate a sweet one (pepper plants in pots at old Baker place) and about selling watermelons when he had his truck (buying a patch of scattered watermelons for three dollars, sold for fifty cents when he got home, buying another patch for eighteen dollars because the grower needed the money to help pay barn help and didn't have time to take melons to the market) and how he used to ride places and see places when he was young, but how he couldn't ride or walk much these days.

January 1985

Winter grass is the color of dirty sheep in a January pasture. I long for greenness. I miss spring plowing, the way it used to be, when I followed my father who followed the plough pulled by the mule, tossing the plough as if beating eggs for a souffle. My father took a deep breath—filling his young lungs with the wonderful spring air and his heart with the hopes of harvest.

Chuck told his mother about a grave in the Chapel Hill cemetery which had a wreath with a pink princess telephone, plastic roses, and a banner which proclaimed "Jesus Called."

VISITING AT GRAMMER AND GRANDDADDY'S HOUSE

Pauline Cheek

When I was eight or nine, and we were heading for the farm from Wake Forest, I would be giddy with happy anticipation until we turned at Dr. Robertson's office onto the North Wilkesboro highway. Then the tension would mount until I became almost paralyzed with dread as we reached the dirt road, passed the Campbells' house, turned right into Grammer's road and left into her driveway. She would be outside by the time we stopped under the cherry tree beside the ivy-covered oak in the side yard, which she swept daily with a homemade broom.

Since I tend to be almost rigid in masking my emotions, I must have felt unresponsive to Grammer as she hugged me to her bosom with a strength that pulled me off balance. Granddaddy would be even less demonstrative than I, remaining seated in his bedroom or on the porch if he were up at the house when we arrived. Then I became the aggressive one and would go up to him to wait for him to take me up on his lap, where I would remain long enough to hear the watch ticking in his overall pocket, or, when I was older, to touch my cheek against his prickly one or to purse my lips in the gesture of a kiss on his bald head, whereon I would note the blue-black mole which brands Daddy's head and mine, too.

This ceremony over, I could relax, spy out all the familiars, including the expected furniture-rearranging in the two north rooms which our family occupied, and begin to enjoy the visit. How much fun it was to have Grammer say at bedtime, "Let me pull down the covers to make sure there isn't a spider in the bed. I'll never forget how Swight was spending the night here one time, and a spider bit him." To lie in the never-never land between sleeping and waking the next morning and hear her come in to build a fire in the stove, or in summer to listen to the cooing doves and the daily crowing contest between Grammer's roosters and the Campbells' and Sharpes', and to smell country ham frying for the early breakfast which Grammer and Granddaddy shared before the rest of us got up; to go with Granddaddy to stake out a goat or shell out corn in the granary; to help Grammer unseat the hens so that we could gather eggs into the big wicker basket with the curved handle; to eat of the special treats which Grammer would put on the table—pickled beets, blackberry jelly or damson preserves, spiced peaches; to glory in her special attention as she showed me her dahlias, cracked out hickory nuts or walnuts on a stone in the yard, or took me to get a dipper-drink at the spring; to have demonstrated over and over that in the eyes of two people we were special indeed. Emotion was powerful—on my part and on theirs—and was welcomed throughout our visit.

But then would come the ritual of departure, and all the pleasure would disappear. Granddaddy would permit us to hug him or— and he seemed more comfortable then—would shake hands and then take off toward the barn or woods. Grammer's face would begin to work, and her eyes grew damp and red. When Daddy had finally gotten the car trunk packed and all four of us locked into the car, Grammer, who would have disappeared during this process, would return lugging a box of canned goods—sausage, tomatoes, berries, pickles, corn— which Daddy would somehow manage to force into the trunk. And when she reached in to the back seat to give Janet and me one more hug and kiss, she would almost apologetically hand us each a jar of something special—honey or our favorite pickle or jelly—which we would tuck in at our feet. Then we would drive away.

NOTHING TO DO WITH GEOGRAPHY   Jane Beed

February 14, 1985, 2 a.m.

Why am I awake—why wake up on this cold a.m. to do this writing? The only warm place in the house is the bathroom so here I sit, on the floor, my back against the sink cabinet and feet propped side by side on the bathtub. Maybe my guardian angel woke me up to tell me something. Anyhow, some things are going around in my head, and if I write them down, they may come out, develop some kind of order that I can work with.

There is snow everywhere. Yesterday a man from the Volunteer Fire Department plowed our driveway, so now we can at least bring the truck down. We would never have been able to dig ourselves out by hand.

The drifts and snowplow efforts have created walls of snow at the Little General store at the lake entrance. The walls are so high that the cars and trucks are hidden. This is the most snow that I can remember—in thirty-seven years. That is a long time. I was eighteen years old, coming from Houston, Texas. There is no snow in Houston, only some ice in the trees in a January storm. There is a warm sun at Christmas and tall poinsettia shrubs at the kitchen door in bloom, exotic flowers of deep red to celebrate the winter solstice.

"Everything is a prologue to this moment." I like that, learned it this summer from a friend. What do we choose to remember, to focus, the foundations of our lives?

Some things I choose not to remember, but they are not forgettable and their residue is a stain or a bitter taste at the bottom of the cup, always.

What is my role and where am I going? Asked that, I know that I'm on a journey—but I don't think it has anything to do with geography. Where am I besides sitting, now crosslegged on the floor of the bathroom?

LOOKOUT   Susan Schmidt

At sunrise, I sit in the fourth-story crows-nest of the old Coast Guard station at Cape Lookout. As the red-yolk sun appears, birds start their noise. I can look at the sun now when it rises, but later it would burn my eyes. The wind is blowing in three distinct keys, the dominant broad swoosh, a low modal moan, and a higher-pitched screech. I am above everything, this barrier island at my feet circumscribed by water in all directions. To the northeast, the Cape Lookout lighthouse across the bight and beyond: Harkers Island; due east is the Atlantic Ocean, all water; south is the Cape point, at low tide; west is Onslow Bay; northeast over the spit in the foreground is Shackleford Banks and beyond is Beaufort, where I lived for three years when I was married.

I have returned for a week in mid-March, ten years later. It is cold, windy and rainy. I return every year. I am staying at the abandoned Coast Guard station with fourteen high school students on a marine ecology trip, half research and half work-service for the National Park Service, which manages Cape Lookout National Seashore. We fifteen are the only people on fifty miles of barrier island wilderness. There is no bridge access to the islands. We came over Monday in Park Service boats. This week we will plant two thousand red cedars and will post signs to keep people from walking across the nesting area for endangered birds. Each student has individual research.

After our first work day Tuesday, planting red cedars on the eastern tip of Shackleford, Keith Rittmaster, dolphin biologist for the North Carolina Maritime Museum, has come to spend the night with us. He and I walk half an hour down the sound beach to see a stranded fin whale, dead for six weeks. We ask the kids who want to see a whale, but they flop around the kitchen, tired from planting trees, and play cards. Approaching from the windward side, I cannot smell the decay of the carcass. Its skin is almost decomposed, so we can see the vertebrae clearly.

Two of the fin whale's jaw bones are already separate from the carcass, and, as they might be washed out by the tide or buried by the sand, we tug the upper and lower jaw bones free from the sand, but they are too big to carry back.

We cut across an overwash between the dunes of the spit and walk back along the ocean beach. I catch sight of the back of a humpback whale as it surfaces to breathe two hundred yards offshore. I watch through my binoculars and count forty seconds between each dive, then pass the binoculars to Keith. We walk along the beach at roughly the same speed that the humpback swims south. After ten minutes, we realize we are watching two whales, and a pod of dolphins that frolic around them. When Keith goes back to the Coast Guard station for his three-wheeler motorbike and trailer, I keep watch, but can no longer see the whales.

At the Coast Guard station, we have a diesel generator for power and lights, which we run five hours at night. In fact, while I am watching whales, the kids are impatient for me to return to start the generator, but it is not dark. They can start cooking, because the stove and refrigerator run on propane. There is an elaborate Rube Goldberg system of battery chargers for twenty-four hour pressure, that breaks down our second day out, so we flush and shower only during generator hours. Back with the ATV, Keith reports that the students do not want to walk the quarter mile to the beach to see the humpbacks. I am disgusted that they are at this pristine beach and don't seem to notice where they are.

After dinner, Keith shows slides of dolphins and whales he has seen around the world. In one slide is a collection of things taken from the stomach of a dead dolphin, including a plastic pen, a lighter, a cigar tip, some metal and plastic fishing tackle.

On Wednesday morning after we finish putting up the signs, I walk along the beach from the spit at the inlet three miles to the Cape point, where waves from Onslow Bay to the west lap against waves from the Atlantic Ocean to the east. I have come to Cape Lookout to find things: ideas, memories, shells, birds. I pick up shells that catch my eye, my idea. Sometimes I retrace my steps to look at one that I have passed, to see its shape: a white wing arched gracefully like a bird wing. After the heavy surf following a week of storms, football-sized whelk shells, called conches in North Carolina, are strewn above the tide line.

I want shells that are perfect, with no holes or cuts on the edge. I find a perfect moon snail, the kind Anne Morrow Lindbergh used as a symbol of serenity in solitude in *Gift from the Sea*. I also find a small helmet, all intact except for some pockmarks. I want bare, naked shells, weathered by the sea, broken or worn to reveal the graceful swirls inside, like the dancing rhythms in Whitman's poetry. I value shells heavy and thick, because thickness shows age and endurance, survival; I value equally paper-thin shells, fragile and translucent. I like whelks with layers worn down to elemental black, or bleached simple, stark white. I want rare shells, seldom seen here out of their tropical range, or the commonest shells like the slick, nacred oyster or the round, white sea scallop, that concentrate right at the Cape point. What I collect the most are weathered surf clams, worn to purple.

Because I walk at water's edge, I take off my shoes and socks, tie the shoe laces at front and back so the shoes ride on my hips. I tuck the wet socks in the laces to dry.

At the Cape point, the wind is coming straight at me at twenty knots. As the tide recedes, the tip of dry sand gets longer. I lean into the wind. It's so shallow, waves break as far as I can see. If the water were warmer than fifty degrees, in mid March, I could wade half a mile out on the shoal. Tonight, a thunderstorm and strong winds are predicted. As the high tide ebbs, a tulip shell glistens, dropped just at my feet by the receding wave, in the overlap between ocean and bay. I discover one sock has dropped, so I trace my footprints, but never find my gray sock on the wet, gray-beige sand.

When I first moved to the coast, just married, I hated the sand, the flat land, the gray mono-color, instead of the green hills and trout streams that I had left. I felt sticky and hot, getting headaches from the glare. All this beach and ocean belonged to my new husband, an oceanographer, not to me. I missed the shade, cool and privacy of green trees. In shock at my mate's infidelities, I sank into shock with little response to senses.

> In a lapse of self-sufficiency
> I marry an oceanographer
> My mother boasts to her friends he is Jacques Cousteau.
> To me the coast is a hot Saturday,
> stalled in traffic on a bridge;
> Like bubble gum blown too big that pops on my face—
> I'm hot with nothing to quench my thirst,
> dirty with no fresh water to wash.
> When we cross the sound to Shackleford,
> we walk through dense forest and dune fields to the beach.
> The air is still except for the buzz of insects.
> I pick off sand spurs stuck in my feet and
> tiny seed ticks crawling up my legs.
> Salt water burns my eyes; sand grates my sun-burned skin.
> I refuse to lie in the dunes when he wants sex,
> I fear someone will catch us naked.

> When colleagues visit from upstate,
> Jacques takes us out to dive on a ship wrecked off Bogue Banks.
> We have to share gear so he takes them all down first
> as I ride the sea swell, alone in the boat with no shade.
> When they roll back over the sides, dripping wet, refreshed and
> sputtering about all the fish they have seen,
> I feel neglected and I want to go down, too.
> Jacques rigs me in black rubber, an air tank and mouthpiece,
> borrowed mask and fins, a man's weight belt.
> I jump over first and sink—overweighted, I sink deep and fast.
> In the murky water I have no visibility.
> I cannot tell up from down
> nor how long I am submerged.

> It's hard to come back from too deep underwater.
> There are no neon reef fish here.
> Underwater is silent and private,
> the absence of sight and sound
> fills me with lethargy and longing.
> My air will not last, so I kick toward the green light
> in the direction I hope is up.
> I only know not to hold my breath to avoid embolism,
> ascending slowly blowing bubbles until I break the surface.

Jacques says he couldn't equilibrate his nose
to come as deep as I was. He wants to blame me.
There is always this distance between us,
the plate glass I shatter when I rise from water to air.

In marriage, I held my breath too long.
When I leave him, a friend takes me to Lookout
to catch bluefish for bait,
like magic, so easy to cast and catch them.
In the surf, I see the wings of cownose rays
slicing the wave of water.
Flying fish skim above the surface, escaping predators.
At the eight-mile buoy off the Cape, where the Gulf Stream
veers in close that day,
Tom beats the water with a boat hook
to call in the amberjack.
They gather excited, the size of sheep,
eager as brides to be caught,
changing colors, yellow, blue-green, iridescent.
I hook one right away, and reel in for twenty minutes,
straining the rod with the weight.
He can hardly hold the eighty-pound fish
over the side for me to see
before he clips the hook to release it.

This is a dream: On a summer morning
while my partner leaves before dawn to fish offshore
I rise slowly to the surface from sleep.
On a waterfront porch, I play my harp
as the dough rises to bake bread.
In the afternoon sea breeze
I sail my sloop to Lookout Bight,
where I anchor and call him on my VHF.
He approaches from the ocean.
We walk across the sand spit halfway to meet, for tea, in the dunes.
I am safe when I sail alone because he listens to my channel.
I can ride the wind in silence 'til sunset; in his motorboat
he can speed to save me if I run aground
am surprised by storm
or am becalmed by dark.

Since catching the amberjack that afternoon, I have seen the treasures at Cape Lookout, and I own them all as mine, especially light on
the water.

ODD-COLORED BUG | Joy Sotolongo

Directly in front of the odd-colored bug, a rectangular panel of sun grazes the edge of the table. The brightest spot gleams in the mid-section, directly in front of me. I crave its warmth on this cold winter day, long to curl myself inside its intensity and become warmed from the outside in. Two black shadows intersect the panel of light, reminding me of the dark patches of thought about impending work that cut into the flow of my writing. Oh, how I resent this other work (my paid work, that is), resent the time it seizes in my mind; how it takes up residence, like heavy furniture; and I find myself first stumbling into it, forgetting that it is there and then taking a long detour around these awkward pieces of concrete thought.

The light in the middle brightens, reflecting a glistening warmth, as I resolve to glide, *en pointe*, around the black thoughts of work, save for one last question: I am the one who placed these obstacles; why is that? To avoid failure, I answer. And now I notice the light has eased on one of the shadows, stretching the rectangle into a longer, more fluid shape.

Metaphors and symbols are everywhere, most often right in front of me, when I choose to look.

I'm looking at the sun beating against the white outdoor table. So bright, this light on white, there are no boundaries; no outline; only a shocking white glare—the sole interruption a lacy network of beech limb shadows. A shocking white glare. The truth eludes me this morning; yesterday; last week. Not truth exactly, but inner peace. I've been thrust into turmoil, or so it feels, for weeks and months on end. I'm inching toward peace by beginning to accept this turmoil. The unknown is slowly metamorphosing from a dark, tightly wound place into a wide open field where anything can happen and, more importantly, something can grow. Where colorful wild flowers can blend into one another, with no particular pattern or order. Just a sea of red and yellow, orange and blue, floating atop a spring-green bottom.

Where anything can happen. Driving to the drugstore last week, I was amazed to spy a tiny bug, a peculiar clear red-brown—the color of sponge coral—holding fast to the windshield. My gaze was drawn to its diaphanous, teardrop-shaped wings that were laced with a delicate network of silken threads. As I watched the wings flutter furiously in the wind, I became astounded, once again, at the strength of delicate creatures. Once again, I think to myself, sitting before the panel of light that now runs the length of the table, obliterating the shadows entirely. What did I mean, once again? Once, I was amazed at the sturdy, circular spider web whose decorative dew-drops dazzled me on a Sunday morning walk. Then there are the children I have taught, whose radiant spirits rose above the desperately hard realities of their lives. Closer. The children.

Because, finally, it was my own childhood endurance and strong will that was touched by the insect clinging to my windshield; I know the feeling of hanging onto an endless and foreign surface that moves furiously forward beyond my control; I've felt my wings huddle close to my body; wings with no choice but to twitch and flutter in a strong, exterior wind, though they longed to open; to send my skinny self soaring above the ground.

This was my childhood. Huddled in bed while an ambulance carried my mother away. Huddled on the basement stairs with my father and his girlfriend while a tornado wreaked havoc outside, my mother's absence louder in me than the winds that knocked down my swing set, that carried my trampoline across the yard.

All the way home, I kept my eyes on the odd-colored bug, and when I slowed down at the end of the drive, it opened its wings and flew away.

INTERIOR WINDOW   Joy Sotolongo

This morning I sit before my interior window. The exterior view is a thin layer of gray. A pale light. Not bright yellow, melting buttery warm sunlight, but a translucent opaque thin-veiled covering.

After reading about myself in my husband's old diary yesterday, I wanted to cry. I mourned the woman he fell in love with, because I am not her anymore. I no longer have my own life, as I did in those days. I have his life. I have the children's life.

I have a small part of work which I love, but must struggle with the friction it causes in my family's life. I have my writing, which has been ignored. I don't give it enough time. I push it. I let it go until it demands I sit down and find myself. Without my writing, I am nothing. Yet, I ignore it. Don't give it discipline. Allow others to steal its time.

It's easy to chastise myself for not writing, but the truth is, I'm running from myself. From one of the most frightening yet challenging processes of all—digging deeper and deeper through the layers to see who or what is there.

This morning, lying in bed, I flew past the childhood I can remember and wondered what's beneath the toddler years, infancy and fetal development. I found something black, cloudy and circular in a soft grand motion. I found peace.

And I found death. Death resides inside. At the bottom of memory. At the inner core. And it isn't frightening. It isn't void or nothingness. It's dirt. Fecund earth. Gritty. Fertile. Damp. Loamy odor. Little tiny balls of dirt that crush between your fingers into a fine dust. It is warm and comforting, like a blanket. Place your cheek on it and it feels cool and slightly damp. A few grains cling to your cheek. You carry them with you throughout the day. Barely aware of their existence, now and then you feel a sticky granule. That is death. We carry it with us, deep inside, a few grains on our cheeks. It is ours.

FAMILY

Once recorders of family histories with much
between the lines, now women ask the questions, who is this family and who am I in it?
Family ties, loose and lovely as satin ribbons or
binding and sere as bailing twine. And
sometimes both. Obligation, affection, the
ambiguous face of heritage. Her role in the
family is paradoxical, and when a woman
writes about this paradox, she helps herself
ravel out the strands, to see love as well as
lures, the liberating force as well as entrapment
and the double bind.

Sometimes escaping into the pages of
her journal can be a retreat from the babble and
hubbub, sentimentality and nostalgia, guilt and
surfeit. Family sayings, family history—our
language is stained with family and so are we.
We are our families. The similarities rise up to
meet us when we least expect it, just as we
think we have put all of that behind us. Why is
southern writing so full of family? Are we
trying to exorcise our families, once and for all?
As daughters, wives, sisters and mothers, there
are expectations that we must bear all, forgive
all, give all. Too much love, or not enough? Can
we ever get it right? We would climb down the
ladder of childhood and run out into the woods
to seek our fortunes. Sometimes it's our journals
we run to. "Journals," says Mary Jane Moffat,
"provide a place to unload, when we fall, a
safety net beneath the wires." Whether birth or

death, housewarmings, anger, loss, holidays, or memories of quiet innocence, the heart finds a journal companion for sharing secrets, without fear of gossip or rebuke.

CALL ME LOVED | Glorianna Locklear

July 10, 1986

 At my mother's house this weekend, I looked at the family pictures she keeps. There is only one baby picture of me. A small black and white snapshot. I am perhaps a year old, sitting in a stroller. My three-year-old sister stands to my right while Aunt Ruth is bending in from the left. Pat is a pretty little girl with long curly hair and is nearly naked, as it is summer in Charleston and very hot. My Aunt Ruth is much larger in the picture than I ever remember her being. A strapping amazon of a young woman with a heavy coronet of dark braids and a billowing cotton dress, dwarfing the baby in the stroller.

 I wear a diaper and a fretful look. Uncomfortable in the heat, which I have always hated. My face is not clear in the small photo, but there is obviously something wrong with the lower half of my face. I know from being told that I had a severe harelip and a nose that had not finished forming at birth, one nostril unfinished. This, naturally, is the reason there is only one baby picture of me, and that one was probably an oversight. There are many pictures of my sister, who was a chubby, pink, blue-eyed infant. There are even the large, hand-tinted variety, still on my mother's walls.

 I also have two brothers, born two years after me. One was stillborn; the other died shortly after birth. I did not realize until recently that my mother still blames herself for their deaths and my deformity. She's not sure how she did it, but she's sure she did. Before we were born she was living a stressful, irregular, constantly upset life. Her family was not thrilled that she had left home to marry a Lumbee, no matter how light-skinned he was. The fact that her babies were blonde and blue-eyed helped a little, but she had no luck in keeping them alive and well. The pain still in her is like a perpetually bleeding wound, and I don't know how to heal it. I think somewhere in her Baptist-guilted soul she thinks the dead babies could be Jehovah's revenge for marrying somebody her folks didn't approve. It would be much better if she could just let go and stop punishing herself. Lord knows the world has punished her enough.

 It is a strange feeling, however, to know I was such an ugly baby no one could bear to look at me, or at least to record their looking. But I have seen cleft-lip adults. They are ugly—no amount of love or compassion can keep it from being so. It's what Yeats calls "the horror of unshapely things."

 My mother was sick for a long while after her two boys died. For a couple of years our little family was scattered—my sister and I in different foster homes. My father was—where? Doing what? No one seems to know.

I must have been an off-putting sight to a foster family and can only imagine how difficult placement was. People were not so enlightened thirty-odd years ago. I have a feeling that I was moved a lot, though I'm not sure why I have that impression. My mother was too bad off to know how we were, or maybe to care. And as far as I know, no one else had the time or energy to inquire.

I suspect the foster homes were pretty poor, as they were almost bound to be at that place and time. My early childhood is a gray blur of misery that never let up. My earliest memory is of a woman with frizzy red-brown hair leaning over me saying, "Her eyes are so pretty, like blue marbles. But isn't it a shame about the rest of her face?" My second memory is sitting on a porch, watching a train go by, feeling trapped, knowing I had to get away or die. Something was definitely wrong, as I didn't learn to talk until I was almost five, and I could never believe the world wouldn't just disappear if I shut my eyes too long. I couldn't sleep much, and still can't. I couldn't speak much, and still can't, though I am learning better how to raise my voice, though the learning is slow, tedious and will be lifelong, I suspect.

The best friend I remember having when I was little was the moon. I heard somebody say something about "the man in the moon," and I took it more or less literally. I thought I saw a benign face, smiling down at me, watching over me. The moonman was my friend who was there sometimes in the day, sailing unbelievably high like a silvery balloon; sometimes at night, his light was visible in whatever little room I slept in. When he was there, I felt there was a part of me that was solid and real too, a bit of moonstone way down deep inside. Maybe it was my Indian blood, my shaman self, that had enough sense to turn to nature for comfort when I was lost in a vortex of sheer misery.

When I was about four I went back to live with my mother. A year or so later my father came back from wherever he'd gone. I thought things would be much better.

I was never so wrong.

July 12

It's 5 a.m., I feel like Jacob must have felt after wrestling with the angels all night: exalted and exhausted. I have been trying to sleep for the last few hours, ever since typing Cabot Worthington's "My Father's Hands" into my computer to keep.

I typed the story into the computer for several reasons. I wanted it to be part of my permanent to-keep stuff. I also wanted to experience the story as fully and slowly as I could. And, in a way, it seemed a service to my father.

I was too tired and overwrought when I finished putting the story in a few hours ago to say plainly how I felt about it, apart from the heartbreaking sympathy and recognition that welled up and spilled out time and again, making it hard to see what I was trying to read and type.

After a night of thinking and dreaming about it all, it comes down to this: I envy Worthington. His love for his father is so clear and plain, and his father's illiteracy is for him another path to loving and sympathy. He wrings your heart because his heart was broken out of the desire to give something he could not. The idea that out of every disaster a seed of new beauty grows is true in this situation. I think it is remarkable for a child to have such complete fellow feeling for a grownup's lacks, and this made the bond between him and his father stronger than it might have been if everything were easier. That kind of love is worth a lot of pain.

I contrast this to the feeling between my father and me, and weep. His being born Lumbee had a lot to do with why he never learned to read at all, and sometimes I feel like a part of the white world that denied him a decent chance at having a good life. I feel that his illiteracy is the linchpin of all the revolving circle of misery and trouble that have mainly made up his life.

The greatest pity of all is that I'm not even sure he recognizes it for the tragedy that it is. Worthington's father had a great desire to read and write, and ached for his lack. I think my father once had a great desire, or at least some, but for years denied it, and I doubt there's much desire left at this point. Indeed, the life he has led has made late learning almost impossible. The fierce drinking and the backbreaking labor which are all he has ever done for work have acted together to shut down his brain prematurely, by way of several "cerebral incidents."

There was a time when the need must have burned hot and painful within him. The best clue I have to this is his reaction to my own reading. When I was a child, I was the only person in my house who read, and I read everything all the time. My father was so massively offended by this that it became the major bone of contention between us. If he came upon me reading, he would often slap the book out of my hand across the room, and sometimes me after the book. His name for me was "four-eyed slut." He claimed reading was making me nearsighted. When he was drunk which was often, he would rant and rave about my thinking I was somebody, always having my face in a book and being too lazy to do real work. He did his very best to prevent me from going to the library, which was the temple of my salvation.

I retaliated, using a child's sharpest weapon: ridicule. I laughed in his face when he hurt me, and made him know he had no real power in the world, that he was just an illiterate bully. I threw it up to him that he was living the only life he would ever have, while I and my books would go somewhere.

I was wrong. I am still there trapped in that squalid little room with him, two people with the same wants and no way to bridge across to each other.

I have spent my life trying to get out of that room, but I sometimes fear the great holes it tore in me aren't mendable. It keeps me from
being able to accept the gifts I have and advances I have made. When
people call me smart, it's like a slap in the face. I want them to call me
loved.

AS WONDERFUL AS A GARTER BELT   Alice Sink

April 17, 1990

As I close my eyes, is there a memory? The camera in my head
focuses on the polio epidemic in the summer of . . . I guess . . . 1950.
Everybody was warned to keep their kids home and not let them play
ball or get too hot or be in crowds. When Momma and Granny went to
town, if I wanted to go, I had to wait in the car with all the windows
rolled up. They would bring me a limeade with crushed ice from
People's Drug. For about a month kids weren't supposed to go even to
Sunday School, so Momma and Granny took turns staying with me. I
told them there wasn't any need to do that, but they did it anyway.

I remember it was lonesome. Nothing to do. Those people
downtown at the newspaper office made it worse by printing that children should rest every afternoon after dinner, eat a balanced diet and go
to bed early at night. Granny also had the idea that it was Coca-Colas
that caused polio so it was a once-a-week treat to get one-fourth of a
juice glass of Coke.

Not permitted to play with other kids I took refuge in the Sears
Roebuck catalogue, especially the pages that showed the ladies' underwear. I never tired of looking at those brassieres, panties and petticoats.
Garter belts were my favorite. I had seen Momma's and Granny's
brassieres and panties and petticoats hanging on the clothesline. But I
had never seen an honest-to-goodness garter belt.

I could not—for the life of me—figure exactly how the thing
worked. It didn't seem to have any leg holes and appeared to be a wrap-
around with elastic straps hanging down to hold the garter snaps. I
turned the catalogue upside down and from side to side trying to get a
better picture in my mind, but I could not imagine. And, of course, I
couldn't have asked Momma or Granny because all I would have gotten
from them would have been a "you'll-know-soon-enough."

I kept my finger tucked in the pages where the bikes and ball
bats were, and I'd flip over quick if Momma or Granny came in the
room. Before the polio ban was lifted, I had progressed from looking to
tracing. With my fingertip, I would outline the underwear, making a
valentine over the top of the model's bosom and down between her legs

and back up over the other side of the bosom to finish the heart shape. Looking straight down my T-shirt, I wondered if I would ever look like the Sears Roebuck ladies.

Momma would come through with a load of freshly dried laundry thrown over her shoulder and, if she noticed anything unusual, she never let on. If I got involved tracing the valentine around the lady's body and Granny walked in, I'd flip to the bike section. Quick. She would say, "Go clean out the tool shed," and that would be the end of the tracing.

One summer evening I was at Aunt Rennie's house. Lying on the living room rug, my head propped up on my elbows, looking at the underwear (Aunt Rennie had a catalogue too, of course). Something like a cloud led me ghost-like up from that living room rug, through the back hallway and up the steep, wooden steps.

Creeping along the upstairs hallway, I stopped outside my older cousin Sarah's bedroom door. Sarah was sitting with her back to me on a stool before a dressing table. I remember every detail. On top of the table were two lamps covered with white dotted-Swiss fabric lamp shades, one on each side. Between lay a silver comb, brush and mirror set. A plastic ear bob tree held pairs and pairs of gold, silver and pearl clips. The dressing table had a stiff white cover that looked like a bride's hat. The wallpaper was flowered. Thin white curtains puffed out over paper window shades.

I could hear cars going by outside the open windows. A dog barked. Lawn mowers sputtered. Birds were nesting in the big maple tree outside Sarah's windows. I stood there in the dimly lit hallway watching Sarah brush her hair, clip on her ear bobs and put on her lipstick, popping her lips together, blotting and then smoothing with a Kleenex. She was getting ready to go to the picture show.

I looked to see if she had on one of those garter belt wonders, but she did not. She wore a crinkled cotton bed jacket at the top and white cotton panties to cover her bottom parts. I should have known from the start that nobody in our family would ever have anything as wonderful as a garter belt.

The sudden slam of a downstairs screen door shook me back to normal. Slowly, I tiptoed back down the stairs and out the side door to lose myself among the dogs, lawn mowers and birds. I vowed that very evening I would someday have me a garter belt. I spat on the ground to seal the bargain.

VISITORS AT THE DOOR | Pauline Cheek

November 3 and 9, 1979

There are Halloweens I remember: Wake Forest before I was ten: Children in stories looked forward to Halloween and had fun on that night. Tobe dressed up and scared neighbors with his visit. I felt that my mother disapproved of children who dressed up and went from door to door. "Begging," she said. I draped a sheet over myself and went out into our front yard, but no one saw me. It was fun to have a jack-o'-lantern, but scooping out the flesh with a spoon so that we would not be wasteful and could have pies was, I found, tedious. And even worse was the discovery that heat from the candle shriveled my happy pumpkin's face and made him smell so that Mother threw him away.

Louisville: Age ten: The long-awaited day when we could move from the two infirmary rooms on the Seminary campus into the house on 158 Pennsylvania Avenue, which Daddy bought from the John R. Sampeys, happened to be October 31. The occupants, the Snodgrasses, had been given three months to find another place, which turned out to be the house next door, so that we had to remove from our minds the resentful thoughts we had against those people who were so slow to get out of our house. Daddy was out of town, and Mother, as usual, had worked furiously to get everything settled and in order as soon as the moving men had left. At twilight, before we had thought about supper, we were introduced to a custom which we had only read about before: trick-or-treaters came in droves, and our initiators, the Snodgrasses, warned that unless people took in trash cans, lawn chairs, even the porch swing, trickers might destroy them. Unprepared, we had to dole out handfuls from the precious bag of peanuts which someone had given us and which we always rationed even for ourselves. Feelings arouse then loom up again each year: uneasiness at not knowing the intentions of the people who parade the streets and suspicions of malicious intent, resentment of anyone who begs, yet scorn at my own stinginess in not wanting to give treats, antagonism against having to conform to society's dictates and in having to give because of social pressure and not because of impulse.

The next year there was added the indecision of whether or not to participate. I, shy, a loner, forever a newcomer or an outsider, an alien in the city, was invited to a Halloween costume party given by a girl I scarcely knew. I was flattered to be included, but scared of the unknown. The easy answer was to say I had no costume. A girl not only offered to lend me a costume but brought it to our Sunday School class meeting. I carried it on the bus and down four or five blocks home, my arms outstretched to balance a box so large they could not embrace it. Inside was a magnificent green satin Spanish gown with a black lace mantilla. How beautiful and sophisticated I felt as I donned it and whirled around in front of the mirror in Mother's bedroom! Then Mother asked, "What will you do at the party? Dance?" I didn't know how to dance. Nobody in our family danced, I was reminded; besides, we were awfully young to be having such grown-up parties, where there might be dancing and no telling what else. My conclusion? It would really be better for me not to go. "Mother won't let me" or "We have plans for that night. I'm so disappointed." I don't remember which lie I told. I felt that my parents were proud of my decision not to go. On Halloween I accompanied Mother as she walked down the street while Janet and her friends rang the doorbell at houses of people we knew and collected bags of goodies. Mother suggested that I dress up in the green costume, but I refused. In the privacy of my room I put on the dress again, but I no longer felt like a señorita.

A HOUSE FULL OF PEOPLE   Anita Skeen

July 8, 1963

I feel today like I've never felt before in my life. I have a feeling of loneliness that I've had only once before—when I came home from church camp in the tenth grade. But this is even worse, and I think it's going to change me. One day I have a house full of people—the dearest people to me in the whole world—and the next day everyone is gone except Greg and me, in an empty house that I never knew would seem so lonely. All this is the truth. I've given up lying. I look at the couches in the dining room and I think Dan and Tim slept here; I look at the book and I think Dan read that story; I look at a chair and I think Dan sat there; I look at a tennis racket and I think that's the racket Tim always beat me with; I look at the car and think of the good times we had riding in it; and I look at my bed and think this is where Aunt Phyllis and Uncle Wick slept. I should be glad to be back in my own room, but I'd give almost anything I own to sleep on that hard cot in the living room with Cindy beside me and Dan and Tim just a few feet away. I can't go on right now. I'll write more tomorrow morning.

These were things that happened that I'll always remember: Tim always complained about the living room clock ticking too loudly so at night he'd take it down off the wall and put it under the couch cushion. He would also go off for a long time by himself and play with Fawn. Dan used to come in those last few mornings and pull the pillow out from under my head. All the times we sat on the front porch. The time we cooked out in the back yard. When we all turned the ice cream freezer. The Monopoly game where Dan won almost everything on the board. How Dan always used to open the doors for me and was really polite about everything. The way we teased each other about having an accent. All the bugs at Appomattox, and how Dan talked about how those boys used to go to Uncle Herb's house to eat dinner. I remember how hard we worked to try to find some rope to take into the woods and make a new grapevine. I remember how we hunted turtles in the lake at Richmond. It's taken me three days to write this, and I have half a page left. I intend to leave the rest of this page in case I think of anything else.

July 11

This has been the loneliest week in my life. When Mother, Daddy and I played badminton Tuesday night, all I thought of was how Dan and Tim and I used to play. It's a terrible feeling of depression. The days are especially bad at breakfast and lunch because then I realize how empty the house is, and I miss having someone to cook the meals. Wednesday night we had a sorority meeting at Doodle Dodson's, and I didn't feel so bad when I was in a crowd of people. They announced about Mary Jane being pregnant and married, and how she couldn't come to sorority any more. I was really shocked when I first heard about her Monday from Susan. I thought she had more sense than that. We talked about rush parties and stuff. I think that, from now on, we're going to have our meetings on Wednesday nights. Today I didn't feel as bad as before. I could even talk about Dan and Tim without crying. I did cry at lunch, though. I got my pictures from their visit back and only five turned out, but I'll send them to Dan as soon as I can. Brooks and I set off firecrackers today. I hope I feel better tomorrow.

TODAY I AM FILLED WITH MOTHER   Judy Goldman

August 27, 1980

Today my room is filled with pictures of Mother.

A formal portrait propped against the wall. A snapshot of her and her younger sister in sun dresses, my mother's arm around Aunt Katie's bare shoulders. A picture that always makes me sad: Mother still able to laugh but already wearing the look of Alzheimer's Disease.

Today I am filled with Mother. I want to swing wide the screened door of her house and shout, "Mother, I'm here!" She'll call, "Judy?" and come dashing into the kitchen with her beautiful smile. We'll hug and touch each other's face as if to confirm the day is here. She will have been ready for hours, sitting in the den smoking a cigarette, waiting for the sound of my car.

We begin with the same dialogue every visit. She asks how the children are, how Henry is doing, and we both settle into the morning the same way we settle into the patterned softness of the sofa. I tell funny stories, and she throws her head back, laughs, and says how bright and delightful Laurie is, how sweet and gentle Mike is. She says how long it's been since she's seen them and how much bigger they probably are now.

Mattie comes in from the bedrooms, and I get up to give her a hug and a kiss. Mother asks me to repeat the stories for Mattie, who laughs and laughs, goes off toward the kitchen talking and lugging the vacuum cleaner.

And the visit goes on. Mother tells me about someone's visit, Frances Jones or Ann Clarkson, and shows me what they brought her. She hands me a pack of mail and other things neatly rubber-banded together. In it, I find a rambling letter from Aunt Fannye, a newspaper article about someone I'm supposed to know, a letter addressed to "Alumnus."

And the visit goes on. She tells me how hard Daddy's been working and how he needs to relax more. I reassure her he looks fine. And the visit goes on.

Oh, how I miss her today. Her love, her softness, her eyes the color of coffee. The comfortable predictability of my visits with her. We were two women who had moved through the mother/daughter relationship to a person/person relationship to a daughter/mother relationship. Each seemed appropriate for the time. Each we accepted as easily as we had always accepted each other.

A MOTHER IN PASSING | Shirley G. Cochrane

January 16, 1983

That last good day we had together, Mother said, "Now if anything happens to me, please don't go around weeping on buses."

And I don't—even when the bus passes Francois, and I see Pierre putting out the umbrellas to welcome this false-spring day. Still, uncontrollable fits of grief strike at unexpected times, in inconvenient places. Not when I open one of her books and a card filled with her familiar handwriting drifts down. Nor when I look through the pictures and find mother-daughter Cassatt poses. Even at the burial service I watched awed but dry-eyed as her ashes were placed in the grave of my father—rib returned to rib cage.

Instead I break down among the Safeway cabbages, her shopping list suddenly blooming inside my head:

3 pink grapefruit
kiwis if available
white seedless grapes w/out brown spots

As I pack up her things, it's the kitchen items that move me most. Especially one crazy little flip-over pan that she fixes asparagus in. The ordinariness of these homely objects dramatizes my extraordinary loss.

January 20

Walking through the Capitol grounds, I realize that Mother will never again watch birds graze on autumn grass. But then she is spared the cruelty of another winter. She will never stand—as she does in my favorite snapshot—with a ruined castle at her back, the green of England at her feet. And yet she was never reduced to riding in a wheelchair. She will never spend another afternoon browsing through books in the Library of Congress. Still, her mind held fast to the last day of her life. And so I move from comfort to loss, loss back to comfort, trying to arrive at a balance.

January 30

How important her things have become to me. Her woolly burgundy hat hangs on my hat rack, her shopping bag with the pyramid of smiling cats, on the knob of my closet door. I keep a pair of her stubby lace-up shoes under my bed. "These are the ugliest shoes in the world," she said once, with a sort of pride. "I fully expect someone to stop me on the street and say, 'Madame, you have on the ugliest shoes I have ever beheld. Wherever did you find such an ugly pair?'" But they look pretty good to me there, peeking out from under my bed.

She often bemoaned my wardrobe, my hair, my shoes—for that matter, my feet, inherited from her. She tended to think that a morning at the beauty parlor, a stylish pair of boots and, most of all, a new coat, could restore me to youth, good spirits, sanity—whatever quality she felt I lacked at the moment. Going over our pictures, I'm struck by the differences in our appearances. She is immaculately coiffed and attired—tiny, raven-haired in the early pictures; in later ones, thinner still and meringue-haired. Beside her looms an obvious daughter (undeniable resemblance) but wearing vaguely neo-hippy clothes, her hair not quite tamed.

Now I'm buying myself zany little memorials to her: a pair of fine leather boots to match her burgundy purse. Next week, a coat, designated in my mind the MWS Memorial Coat. A slightly extravagant coat, one I don't really need but that will lend me a touch of elegance.

February 1

I try not to store up what John Updike calls "guilt gems." But I do have certain regrets. I wish I'd been more patient. Oh, I never screamed or railed or said things that lie like stones upon the heart. Rather, it was a sighing wind of impatience. It had to do primarily with pace—hers increasingly slower and with a sometimes maddening leisureliness. A stroll around the hotel room when I would be wildly packing to get us off on the next lap of the journey. A long gaze into a shop window as our bus panted up to the metro stop. I see us: me at a come-on, come-on angle; she, small and elegant, walking as though she were admiring the boxwood of an English garden.

And her deafness. Scenes like this: I'd say: "M. has had a lot of losses this year." A look of horror would cross (Mother's) face and she would ask: "M. has had a lot of lawsuits this year?" Whereupon I'd throw myself back in the chair as though hit by an arrow, muster my forces, lean forward and shout: "Losses, losses, losses." "Oh yes, oh yes," she'd say, never chiding me. That last day in the hospital, when we had our good, long talk, I was sitting slightly behind her head as she lay in bed, and this was the perfect angle for her to hear every word.

When I was at a village tea room in Kent, I observed a middle-aged man out with his aged mother (she wore a bonnet exactly like a baby's Easter one, tied under the chin with ribbon). The man leaned forward and asked: "What would you like for pudding (dessert)?" A blank look. He tried again: "What would you like for pudding?" When I left, he was still slowly repeating the question. I wish I could have had some of his patience.

And why wasn't I more affectionate? I was never a great mother kisser or hugger, even as a child. Was it because I felt deserted as a baby, when she had to turn me over to Granny for those first few weeks, when I never saw her? I've never felt any great need to thrash out this question on an analyst's couch; I just note it in passing.

But why did I not at least tell her I loved her? Every night she used to call Granny at the nursing home to say, "Don't forget how much I love you." Why was I so stingy with that word love?

But I remember something: on that final perfect day we had together, I said, "We must hurry up and get you well so we can find some new exciting places to have lunch. There's no one I like to go to lunch with as much as you." She must have recognized this as the reticent's version of "I love you."

February 15

What I mourn now is not her death—a release, after all—but the pattern of her life. That last good day in the hospital, she said,

"You've plowed a straight row." I protested, "Look at all my zigzags, my dead stops, my turnings back."

"But on the whole," she insisted, "you've plowed a straight row."

Life forced a zigzag pattern upon her, but miraculously she too plowed a straight row.

NIGHT IS THE HARDEST TIME OF ALL   Amy Wilson

January 5

    Yesterday evening the sun was down
    but through the blinds
    the moon made a shadow on her chin
    I had to make sure it was a shadow
    I waved my hand through it in front of
    a finally sleeping face

January 6

    She says, "Always do the best you can"
    So tonight, Ma, I am alone
    Did I tell you that I cleaned my house today
    I mean I used the pine cleaner
    and I scrubbed the floor
    on my hands and knees

January 8

    Overcast, some wind
    I have errands to do today
    but I'd rather see you

January 10

    Last night I got drunk
    as if I were a child
    Mama, I'm sorry
    I danced and I sang and people drove me
    home safely now

January 11

    A candle burns near a sunlit window
    I watch the flame and I know its warmth now
    Yesterday, Susie and I worked together to walk you
    Now it takes two of us

I saw the covered pain in your face Susie
I felt the uncomfortable pain again
Why is she suffering

A woman friend named Grace
knocks, walks in softly
Ma is sitting up in the chair by the bed
This woman has something, I think,
the way she moves
One of the first of your religious friends, Ma
that does seem truly sincere and caring to me
She reads you Psalms and when I go out
for a moment she begins a prayer
She even throws in a word for me
I told Grace that I am to meet with him
I know that it is to tell him
that there was a baby
and he was the father
and the baby's gone now

January 13

The sun is shining through the Venetian blinds.
I wish you were home with me
The hardest thing about this is that
I do not want to remember
you as a sick woman
I make up my mind—
the good times
the jitter-bugging times

February 2

Today
it snows lightly
as it did the Friday
that we brought you home

I find myself holding your hand more
just standing beside your bed
Yesterday you were not satisfied
with a room of your own
(Does it get lonely now?)
So I pulled the wheelchair up
and sat by your bed
as you attempted to watch cartoons
and I held your hand

Do you see the snow
or will you want the curtains
open today

February 8

This morning
after Renae woke me at five a.m.
to check you because you were in so much pain
and I went back to bed after standing by you
and telling you to be quiet and just sleep
This morning after walking back down the hallway
in the dark and climbing into a warm bed—
your warm bed—I dreamed that you were dying

February 18

His name was Lil Willis
You used to jitterbug
Nights and cool Mississippi—
nights in a row spent with him
"We kissed and necked
but he was engaged and from out of town
from the beginning.
He wanted me to meet his parents
I'll never forget that"
"What did you tell him, Ma"
"I told him I didn't want to
It wouldn't be right
He was marrying someone else
He couldn't break off an engagement
of a whole year"

February 21

You sleep with a fast respiration and pulse
Is that you in there
I've been going through family pictures
like a scavenger
One of the pictures seems beautiful and odd
You stand in a pose like a model
The wind blows your dress
You seem strangely thinner
Legs slim and feet in brief but heeled sandals
Hair soft, sensual knowing upon your face
Maybe this was taken when you dated Lil
the blond, tall, blue-eyed, already-engaged boy-man
with whom you used to dance, dine and neck

Lil Willis—where did you say he was from, Ma
This photograph is singular
this stance
It must have been with Lil, Ma
and I think I'll wait till I feel that way—to know

| ANGER AS OLD AS MY HURT | Lynn Bunis |

January 18, 1978

How old is my anger?

It's as old as my hurt.

It's as old as the little girl's anger. I can see her—have always been able to see her. I'm standing behind her, perhaps in the doorway to the room. The little girl's back is to me. She is suspended in anticipation. Something is about to occur. Her mother is not in the room. But the little girl knows she will be in the room very soon. I see the child in a blue dress. The dress is so short that the little girl's panties show. Her legs are chubby and pink. She is halted in motion—perhaps one hand touches her tousled curls. She's alone in the room and she's vulnerable. And she has just been hurt or she is about to be hurt. I am not sure.

Her mother suddenly grows angry. Something the child has done has caused her mother to become very angry. Her mother's face screws up. Her mother's eyes narrow. Her mother's nostrils flare. Her lips, her mouth grow rigid. The little girl looks and she knows something has happened. She must have stepped out of babyhood into childhood. She must have just then crossed that threshold where she was going to be taught that she was accountable for her every action.

Her mother says something to her. "Just you wait!" or "Don't you move!" Something like that. And her mother angrily stalks out of the house. Out the front door. The screen door slams with an awful smack. The little girl stands trembling, feeling bewildered. Something has happened. Something beyond her control and yet she is being held accountable. She is just learning what this means. She is being taught this this very moment.

The mother comes back into the room. She's carrying a switch. Her hand is so tight around the thick end of the switch that her skin has gone white. Her movements have gone jerky. Her elbow is held very rigid; the arm extended from the shoulder in a rigid crook.

Does the child look in the mother's face? I can't remember. I can only see the mother's arm and then the other hand that reaches out. It grabs the little girl just below the little blue puffed sleeve. And suddenly the mother grabs the child's arm and, with the other hand, she moves that switch rapidly, stinging the child's legs and the child is dancing. And the child is crying because suddenly she is being switched by her mother who has always given her nothing but love and affection. And the child has never had this happen to her before. Her mother has turned on her! The one person with whom she has spent every waking moment, who has bathed her, and fed her, and woken her lovingly, sung songs to her, played games with her. She's unleashing a fury—on the child! And the child doesn't know why!

It hurts! She wants it to stop. She's screaming. She's shrieking. I don't know what she's saying; whether she's saying, "No! Stop," "I'm sorry," or "Mother!" I don't know what she's saying.

The mother becomes overwrought. She has never done this to her child. She looks down at the little face which is red and distorted, horror-struck, hurt and crying. And she says, "Oh!" And so she has to say, "Don't you ever do that again." (Does she think naively that the child is going to be so traumatized by this occurrence that she will never again do anything wrong? That she will suddenly gain a sophistication that even grownup people never get—where they will always think of the consequences first, instead of the delicious temptation of an act or an utterance?) The mother says, "Don't you ever do that again." And she means, "Don't ever make me do this again! I can't stand what I've done! I can't believe what I've done! I didn't even know I knew how to do what I've done."

The child knows immediately that the mother's anger has abated, fled away from her as swiftly as it came. And with just as much reason, as far as the child is able to discern.

THE LIVING MAN   Nancy Markham

August 18, 1976

Me: Daddy, I don't know what to call you. The part of you I'm talking to is my father; but the time in my life that I was able to talk to you was before I was twenty-eight. You were Daddy to me then.

F: I am your father no matter what you call me.

Me: I know. You gave me life where it matters to me—my mind and my spirit, my feelings of myself and my sensitivity to others' pain. They haven't made life easy for me but that's okay; I've got another half of life to live where it will be more acceptable.

F: When you were in graduate school I began to get worried. You were doing exactly what I had seen you doing, what I wanted you to do, what I had prepared you to do and you weren't happy. You had come from New York emotionally almost demolished and I waited and hurt to see the pain of your losing your fiance. I thought then that you must want those things that women seem to want. Then you decided to go back to school to study literature. It was too good to be true. I didn't dare show you how happy I was.

Me: I remember your standing at the kitchen door ready to go to work. I said something about going to school at Wake Forest in the spring. All I could think of was that learning had given me a base for healing my wounds before. College could do it again. You stopped very still for a moment and acknowledged that that could be arranged. You didn't show much feeling but I knew you were pleased. I knew what would please you and I couldn't think of anything else to do. Now I see that it wasn't quite accidental. That was the path I had to take.

F: But it led you to graduate school instead of just a teaching credential and that worried me.

Me: You and Mama said you almost suggested I give it up. I'm so glad you didn't. What would I have had without it?

F: I really don't remember saying that at all.

Me: If I was doing what you wanted me to, why didn't you participate in my graduation? I know, Charlie got his B.A. on the same day. Just like you and Uncle Tom got your M.A. and B.A. on the same day. I pushed too hard to get through the thesis and the orals so I could do that because I thought it would mean something to you. You could have told me I didn't have to rush. That would have relieved the pressure and still given me my degree. I had forgotten to notice that you and Uncle Tom both got your degrees at Duke in the same exercise; Charlie and I were at two different colleges. I realize that you were included in his commencement; you were big cheese.

F: I'm sorry about all that. I didn't know it would mean so much to you.

Me: I'm really off the track I started on. I'm talking about the accoutrements of outer wisdom, and your real gift to me was inner wisdom. You taught me about giving and as much as you knew about loving. But I really appreciate you most for giving me the power to develop my thinking process.

F: I didn't give you that; you had it in yourself. You were able to respond to that part of me. Charlie didn't respond to that. I was the same father to him.

Me: I don't think you were. I think you were soft with him. You expected much of your first born and I've tried to give it to you, until sometimes I don't know where you stop and I start.

F: I guess, as you say, I stopped when you were twenty-eight; you kept going. You are still going.

Me: And I want you to go, too. Those two years after retirement I saw your mind and spirit die; I knew the body would be next, and it almost was. After touching death you came back; it's like you have new life—why not new wisdom? Follow with me. You gave me your wisdom as my life began; let me give you my wisdom as your life ends.

F: I invited you to share most of your spiritual development with me last summer. You were going to tell me about yoga. You never did.

Me: I got so tired of your intellectual argumentativeness—that very quality that so stirred me during Sunday dinner sermon analyses, now turns me off.

F: Those Sunday dinner talks were really important to you, weren't they?

Me: You treated my comments seriously even when I was five years old. Most men do not do that, even now that I'm a university teacher. I thank you for taking me seriously.

F: You were a serious child.

Me: I'm still a serious adult. Does it make sense that I have fun being serious? I rather resented Daniel's sermon last week implying that ascetic life could not give heights of joy. It can.

F: Is that really true for you or are you just copying my inability to have fun? I have spent years justifying that.

Me: You have fun at circuses and picnics and entertainments, don't you? I remember you had fun with the family, or you seemed to. That's sort of like me, too. I'm most happy when I'm doing non-serious things with people I love, otherwise why bother?

F: Is that why you can't dance again, because you haven't found people you love to dance with?

Me: Maybe, I danced at church with people I hardly knew but there was the kinship of our union. I danced at the women's dance. Kinship again.

F: I had a hard time letting your mother persuade me to let you have dancing lessons. It was against my religion.

Me: I'm so glad you did. You finally even gave three hundred college women the privilege. Thanks to Mama and the fact that I hadn't turned into a devil.

F: What has all this got to do with wisdom? Is it the wisdom of the body to dance?

Me: To dance and to make love. You know that part, you lusty old man.

F: Not anymore I'm afraid.

Me: Maybe not in the old ways. I bet the thoughts are still there. I never had the sense that you used your sexuality or that you ever hurt because of it. Is that another way that I've idolized you?

F: Perhaps, but if it gives you strength to do that by all means go ahead. It's your mother that has to live with the real me.

DEATH DETAILS | Jane Hanudel

July 24, 1978

He is dying. He has deep brown eyes, and they contrast so starkly with his white hair, his pallor, the white sheets. His eyes are quiet, they do not complain. He stares evenly, deeply, quietly. His hand often crooks over his head, rests on his hair. He is solemn in bed. He turns from side to side. When he sits up, which is infrequent, he looks worse; he looks more comfortable when he is lying down. When he sits up, he suffers shortness of breath, a symptom which he tolerates less than the weakness. He sits up, gets up with the help of a walker, sits for a while, gets a glass of water, drinks it (and his hands shake), then goes to the bathroom or lies back down. He has been in bed for more than two weeks now. He has not been to his office. I think now of his office; how dark it must look, how much perhaps some of the secretaries miss him.

His realm is the bed. Occasionally, Dad goes into the den and sits in the velvet recliner. He lets out a deep breath upon sitting down— falling back to the point you think the chair will fall backwards. He sits there and reads the paper. I suppose he is waiting for death, patiently waiting. He still wishes for something, anything, that will make him feel better, make him rid of the disease. But the cancer is winning. The disease was held in check for awhile, but it came back stronger and more relentless. And he bowed under: he had to, he had nowhere else to go.

July 25

Mom is working out the death details. Today she purchased two cemetery plots for $380. She brought home mimeographed, stapled sheets explaining all that was necessary to know in purchasing a cemetery plot. She laid the set of papers on the kitchen table and sat down and wearily said how hot and humid the day was. She had walked around the cemetery; it took a long time. This was something, she explained, that would be well near impossible to get done after the death. These are things that are so much better worked out early— worked out before the dying. In order to plan the funeral and order the monument, you must make an appointment. I asked her when this would be done. She said she would try to do it tomorrow. I wonder when her steel will crack, when her inner workings will start getting mixed up, not meshing well. I pray that the time will occur after my father is dead—if indeed it does occur—which I realize could happen yet I hope it does not.

Mom sounds tired as she goes through the days: her world is restricted to the house, the bedroom where Dad is, the greeting and visiting with company. I feel Mom is suffering through this. You say: fool, any wife would—or most wives would. This one does I believe share a greater burden of anxiety than others—particularly those others who will be well cared for after the death of the spouse. Mother is afraid, I think. She wonders about the details of social security, pension, benefits of retirement. She doesn't show these worries or burdens. She chats with company, keeps up a fairly staunch attitude of practicality—attention to the mechanics of getting through life tasks. In talking with me tonight, while the two of us shelled butter beans, she mentioned to me her desire that Dad not retire, that he remain superintendent (of schools) as long as he can—until age sixty-five. If he died "in service"—while still in the superintendency, she would receive a respectable amount of money. If he died in retirement, she would not receive this. This situation angers me in that I have reason to believe Dad is leaving the "to retire or not to retire" question up to the school board—in what he termed "make the decision in the best interests of the school system." To me that's an insensitive way to go. Mom deserves every penny she can get.

July 29

The house still stands, a house filled with all the normal things, and also housing death. Mother came in today and stood in the washroom area in order to tell me about the death details. She spoke hushed a bit. She did not want Dad to hear. She has arranged everything with the funeral home ahead of time. Everything from the order of the family entering the church to the question of the type of container Dad should have to be lowered into the ground. A vault or a plain pine box? The casket arrives (when ordered I suppose) in a plain pine box. The pine box is cheaper, and we both prefer it.

There was not much emotion in Mom's voice as she described to me the procedure she went through at the funeral home. She spoke in soft, serious tones. She wore a black and white checkered dress; her hair, quite gray now, seemed to blend with this dress. Her face was serious, eyes tired and a deep color blue. She has got it all behind her now; she has taken care of the death details.

August 17

Dad is worse. He is dying. Tonight Dr. Brown took him off all medication. He was more uncomfortable today than on previous days. Tonight I went onto the back porch to talk to Mother about it because she feels she cannot give me answers over the phone. I came back into the house alone after having spoken to her briefly. I came into the kitchen. As I entered the kitchen, I felt death in the house. I walked more softly, more carefully because I might knock the death winds, might disturb them. I felt—

I went into Dad's bedroom. He was uncomfortable. He let out small groans, grunts now and then. He lay on his back. His face was white. He looked uncomfortable. He asked about his pain medicine. Mother quickly came to the bed and figured out what he needed to have—what and when. He would need his next pill at three a.m. I think about Mother getting up in the night—at three a.m.—to administer his medicine. I think about her realizing the darkness outside, thinking that in a few hours it will be morning—and that another day begins again: with food, cleaning, visitors. I think about her not being able to sleep after getting up, how tired and worn she must be—after all of that. And then to get through the day, in worry and in anxiety, through the visitors and through the loneliness, through all kinds of things—to return to the night—to the time when others sleep without interruption.

THE SAFETY OF MY OWN ARMS | Kristin Petersen

Bruce is gone again, this time to a mountain on the west coast of California. And I am here, waiting. So far I have felt good during this pregnancy, but now all sorts of uncomfortable symptoms seem to be plaguing me. Hot face, dry eyes, persistent cold and cough, legs that don't want to hold all of me up when I first wake up. I tire easily and am again worried by stomach cramps. Swimming used to get all the kinks out. I felt free and light while stroking through the water. But now, as my head submerges, I feel claustrophobic with the thoughts that come crowding in—wondering when 'it' will happen, and whether Bruce will be here or not. My body feels very aware of the little ball of life bound to my stomach. As I swim, it seems to keep trying to come to the surface. Stroking through the water, turning my head to the side for air, I feel the pulling on my belly.

* * *

Rachel nursed three times last night and relieved my fears about whether she would be okay or whether I was really starving her. Afterwards she cried in that angry "I'm hurting" way and Bruce held her and was bewildered and upset about what to do. Finally she settled, occasionally opening those seas of blueness to look at me—somewhat reproachfully it seemed.

Bruce went down and got us each a coffee, and then he left and I wished for him to be here always. It is grey outside and as I look out I realize what a protected little place I'm in here. It's as if weather and my whole other life have ceased to exist.

* * *

I awoke in a hospital dawn and settled myself in anticipation of the baby's arrival to nurse. My breasts felt warm and expectant but still there is no milk. I listened to the cries of babies being wheeled down the hall and tried to hear a familiar cry as the squeak of the bassinets rolled by my door. When the nurse comes she always matches the number on Rachel's wrist band with the one on mine. This amuses me. I will always know her tiny face from the others. I watched as she came from my body and in the moment it took for my eyes to rest on her small self I had memorized her for keeps. Today I go home.

* * *

A Sunday afternoon seven weeks after Rachel's birth. The experience of childbirth is so phenomenal and so unexpected and so earth shattering—I had no real preparation for it at all. I planned to write about each feeling as it emerged, making it crystal clear for new mothers to come. But the days slipped by and I am left with retreating memories, mere reflections of reality. Still, seven weeks is closer to birth than seven years. So I'll try to reach back to the rawness of each new moment.

First, the blood. Somehow I didn't think about how much blood there would be afterward. I said to Bruce right after we were left alone, and I held an ice pack in place between my legs—"Bruce, I'm bleeding. You'd better call the nurse." And all he said was that I was supposed to bleed. That statement was to be the beginning of a whole new reality. To be in a strange room away from home in all your nakedness, dripping blood and holding ice in a cloth between your legs—and that was the way it was supposed to be.

It's not how to take care of the baby that is so overwhelming. It's how to deal with all the new feelings inside of you that is so overwhelming. I am not depressed, but I think about the baby and imagine something happening to her and it makes me cry. I can't seem to accomplish anything but seem to be always busy. I am upset with Bruce for smoking near the baby but then am upset with myself for being upset. I feel protective of her, of me, of Bruce, of us. I become fiercely possessive of the "us." Bruce and I murmur over the baby, over each other; our heads together, murmuring. My vagina and bottom hurt—ache, throb, feel heavy. I am seized with the dawning realization that my life will never, can never, be the same. I mourn my lost life at the same time that I celebrate my new one. Never once do I wish the baby away.

I envy, resent, feel sorry for myself because Bruce has so easily slipped back into his old life while I lay stranded here on this unknown stretch of sand with no hope of ever getting home again. I find little evidence that I will be able to build a new life that can include work, play, friends and Bruce; that can be as satisfying as the one I so innocently gave up. Bruce comes to visit me on the sandy strip, but he doesn't really live here with me. He is part of a bigger world, somewhere else. My world feels shattered, not like broken glass, like a prism in a kaleidoscope; the same familiar pieces shifting into a new pattern that is still alien to me. I am in the center of a new reality, a different focus on the same old world.

* * *

I thought it was Rachel who brought me a lovely newness. But now, with Bruce out of town, I see that it is his and my joint reflection of her, our joy of watching her between us, that brings the loveliness.

* * *

Yesterday Rachel was out of sync with her world. She didn't hurt, only needed to be held. It was a holding day. And I told her, "There will just be days like this. They just come, but they also go again and that's the way it is." I didn't want to tell her that I'd wish the bad times away if I could. I don't want her to think that the bad times are something to hide from because I know she needs both ends to hold her center in place. So I give her a holding day, and I feel along with her a bit to comfort myself; and I let her have her downs.

* * *

It is a sultry spring evening. My arm aches from propping up my sleeping baby who cried herself to sleep on my shoulder. Bruce is out of town and it is quiet here. A friend of mine lies dying in the hospital. The setting sun turns the brick wall outside the window a dull gold. I feel the baby's relaxed sleeping body, warm against my shoulder, see her tiny bare foot limp on my chest. There will be a new moon tonight.

MORE VALUE THAN SPARROWS | Katerina Whiteley

Maria, fourteen, healthy and beautiful, wakes up and asks, "What's for breakfast?" with all the assurance that she will be fed. I cook a large breakfast, since it is her vacation and her favorite meal. My heart says, "Thank you God that I can feed my child," but my eyes fill with tears.

I serve father and daughter as they read. Before they can see my eyes, I excuse myself and run out to the yard to rake. For I have remembered the cause of my anger, which now slips into depression. Last night we went out with friends to eat, but I could not touch the food. I had just listened (I, the coward, could not *look* at television) while Tom Fenton's cultured voice recounted the tragedy of those devastated lives in drought-stricken Africa and did not hide our government's complicity in sending arms, not food, to the third world.

And now, this morning, I feed my own child, but the guilt that I cannot feed the others, the starving children, becomes unbearable. My tears run crazily down my cheeks and wet the ground. Suddenly the rake stops, as of itself. An empty nest lies on the grass. I approach carefully. Even the birds, I think bitterly. But when the blurring of my eyes eases, I see the tiny shells, neatly cracked, parted in two. The birds have hatched. "Are not five sparrows sold for two pennies? And not one of them is forgotten before God. Why even the hairs on your head are all numbered. Fear not, you are of more value that many sparrows."

I am glad he didn't say *all* sparrows.

December 29, 1980

I'm at the point of life now when years don't have that specific separateness of the years of my youth. There was a time when the events of my life were distinguished by the number of that year. In 1960, we lived in Massachusetts. In 1964, Rudy was in Vietnam. In 1959, Niki was born. Now they all run together. The events into years, the years into events.

I know this is a sign of advancing age. The galloping away of years. But why? Why does it happen so? Is it the repetitions of experience? In our childhood, each year brings a new experience as knowledge advances. But now—is knowledge so stale? That would be a pity.

January 2, 1981

At Sugar Mountain. A charming condominium set in a dip, near the slopes. All my children have just walked out to go to the slopes for their first day's skiing. Rudy, rather irritated, as he usually is when he has to wait for so many people; Michael, a nephew, who is so different from my girls, because he doesn't know how to entertain himself; Maria, rather smashing in her blooming girlhood at fourteen; Niki, very happy because she's in love; and G., who is like her in looks, but so excitable, different from Niki's innate quietness, bringing a new dimension to her life, changing her. At first, I resented this. Now it amuses me.

There are bare branches in front of me. Their right sides are touched with a layer of snow. Now the wind blows away and little tufts dislodge themselves gently, reluctant, and float through the air. Patches of blue sky amidst white clouds, a pastel, tender blue, the sun occasionally blesses parts of the land, and, as I write, it mocks me and shines fully for two seconds, making the view glisten, then glances off again.

January 16
Went to Greenville with Maria to shop. I have such a difficult time communicating to her the need for control of "fashionable" expenses. And yet, she is so touchingly grateful and sweet when I get her what she wants. What is the right way to train her? "Patience is a bitter cup which only the strong can drink."

January 17
Niki left at 5:00 p.m. for New York. She called at 11:00 to tell me they were okay, getting ready to fly to Spain at 1:00 a.m. I spent a restless night, waking to pray. Reached point of exhaustion the next day.

February 20
Rudy's birthday today. Forty-seven years old. We are both aging. Why is this always a surprise? He and I work every night on "The Fantastics." It's beginning to take shape.
Maria is at "all-state" today. Calm and still surprised at her win (she is a majorette). She is a dear child. A tremendous comfort to both Rudy and me. Started an essay today. As usual, what comes out is different from what I intended.

April 21
The book of quotes is blank on this day.
Blank. That's how I feel. But Niki writes from Spain, wonderful vignettes, captured on the back of postcards. Maria has a vacation this week and what a joy and comfort the child is. She plays a beautiful piano, strong-fingered and accurate. What a pleasure to hear it.

June 11
Left for Spain.
Seeing Niki is the first objective. She is thoroughly well-organized and beautifully efficient. Madrid brought back memories of Niki at five, of my Eros for Rudy, my first bitter fear and disappointment, and then, here is this tall, slender twenty-one-year-old daughter, speaking Spanish fluently and guiding us expertly.

July 10
Niki talked to the University of North Carolina today and got the news that she was accepted at graduate school and, as I hoped, really believed, she has received a fellowship to teach one class this semester . . . Great joy! After all the fellowships I gave up to get married, I am glad my daughter can teach in college.

July 14

Today, Niki had another offer of a fellowship from Florida State University. And here she is, my child, with two offers, as I had twenty-three years ago. I opted to marry her father. Did I look into the future and see this exact scene?

July 16

I am reading Madeleine L'Engle's *The Irrational Season*.

Whenever I read her books I think—yes, this is exactly how I think and feel, without her intellectual superiority and discipline. Why did I come from a background that said girls should not have ambition, work hard, excel? Why is my energy so limited? Why am I so undisciplined?

God help me to get on with my writing, to get it all down before I die.

August 10

On Saturday afternoon after I took Roberta an offering of love, I ran into an insult of impersonal meanness. I got a speeding ticket, that close to home, after having driven 1500 miles! I felt terribly angry. But then I went home and read Martin Niemoller and realized that in such *small* acts, one learns to be non-violent.

September 22

Also, I get so upset that no one takes these hours I slave here seriously. If you write, you don't work. Bad dream last night about J. R. losing her youngest. Why should I dream that? And I am so depressed about B. S. (a neighbor dying with cancer) and his condition. I had a stark feeling just for a second in the shower that the whole thing is really meaningless. What do we really know? And then the anchor came: *Christ was and is.*

September 22

The news just came that Roberta's son died last night. I find it impossible to believe. Did I feel her agony last night? Is that why I dreamed? God, have mercy. Christ, have mercy. Lord, have mercy.

September 29

I came home to find my little Bridget (our wire-haired fox terrier) dead. My heart is sick and sore inside me. Death is stalking. I am sad, so sad. And little Maria is so broken. Only Niki doesn't know our sorrow. What do we do wrong? (It is the second dog we have lost.) I am sore at heart. Oh, God protect my children. Life is so suddenly fragile. I am filled with sorrow.

October 15

I went to Chapel Hill to see Niki. Chapel Hill was lovely with exquisite fall colors and mellow sun. Niki asked me to go to her class. She teaches very well—full of enthusiasm. I love her—this child, this *other* I helped create, so separate from me yet mine in her sorrows and joys.

November 4

My precious Maria is fifteen—an age I remember as so troubled, painful. She is prettier than I ever was, she is lovely, and yet so much younger than I was then. Isn't she? Delighted her with something very simple—just a dinner for some of her friends.

November 18

Niki's birthday.

I've listened to Brahms' symphonies, especially the third, that gorgeous sound I listened to on November 18, twenty-two years ago, that last day of my life, ever, when I was still Rudy's and my own, with that peculiar freedom (selfishness) that exists when you have not yet given birth, before your life becomes bound through eternity to the child of your womb.

LOVERS, HUSBANDS AND FRIENDS

As roles change and rules change, journals are the place where blurred thoughts can become focused, feelings can gain clarity. The admonition to not put asunder refers to the hundreds of little daily assaults and body blows inflicted by one against another. Friendships, erotic or not, smooth or not, soften the sharp edges of public life and clarify the cloudy waters of private life.

Journals record and sift the ups and downs of finding and losing friends, mending fences and pulling up stakes. They chronicle deep affection for friends just made and friends we have had forever. At times, journal entries are substitutes for letters to friends we would like to mail but can't.

We want to treasure the days when a phone or a visit or a trip together renew our friendships. The roller coaster of erotic, as well as that of familial love, needs to look out on the more serene landscape of friendship.

RICHER BECAUSE OF OUR CROSSINGS | Jamie Tevis

June 25, 1984

As I went down the walk, I knew that it was hopeless for me not to be affectionate toward the people who came through my life. I came to realize that the pain of parting is a bittersweet sorrow, because my life was richer because of our crossings and a thousand times better than the dull depression I had once felt. I agree with Aristotle that living together, or in close proximity, is important to good friendship, because when we live with someone, we can give the gift of time that is so scarce in our busy lives.

June 28

Sarah from Los Angeles led the first class discussion on Aristotle, and she took us quickly into the question, "How does lifestyle affect friendship? Can the rich be friends?" Brian told how his friend had gone to California and gotten into a relationship with a girl friend, who was running in the fast lane with movie stars and drug users. Judith thought that perhaps the man could not accept the girl's way of life even if the girl accepted his. Aristotle says that friends are friends as long as they have something in common and the more things in common the better the friendship. Someone said that friends are for therapy, the sharing of problems.

I disagree, because my friendship with Madelyn Cavanaugh was the best of my many friendships. It was friendship, in the C. S. Lewis sense, in that we did things together through the years, side by side but looking outward. When I tried to tell her about the pain of my marriage she said, "I don't know what you are talking about and cannot share this with you." It was her honesty and her sense of her own self worth that made her a good friend for me. It was therapy for me to be with her, because I always felt better after spending time with her, even if we didn't discuss my problems.

I believe as the song says, "You must walk this lonesome valley. You must walk it by yourself. Nobody here can walk it with you. You must walk it by yourself." I have been through a divorce and I have seen other people go through the same pain but no one can know and feel the pain completely for another person. I would not want a friend to have to feel the same hurt. What I need is someone to love me and to wait for me to recover, while I am raw and suffering inside.

I looked across the table at Caroline and the thought struck me that what kept her teaching in frigid Alaska was warm friendships.

Margaret and I have been like two college freshmen getting our house in order. We made a list of things we needed and took off to Mount Vernon as soon as class was over, ate a quick lunch and then found the Goodwill store. She got a lamp with no shade, a glass for pencils and coat hangers. I got a pan, curtains for Helen, and a mug for Ron. At K-Mart, Margaret found a lamp shade, a radio, and I got a yard chair for sunning myself. We filled our grocery list, adding frozen TV dinners. I introduced her to the joys of Odd Lots where I got a popcorn popper and she, a fifteen-cent soap dish. We found six posters to brighten our upstairs salon, which we reach by a winding, wooden staircase.

We fancied ourselves Gertrude Stein and Alice B. Toklas getting ready to entertain the budding young writers of the community, as we took great pains to hang our gorgeous posters, just right, over our two couches. Admiring our work, we went downstairs to read Cicero for tomorrow's assignment. Hunger pangs struck, and I climbed the stairs to try out my new toy, the air corn-popper. As I hit the light switch, I felt a bit sad that Margaret couldn't share this fun with me, as she had told me earlier that she couldn't eat popcorn. I took a bowl of it to her room to show her that the popper really worked, and she took a handful to please me.

July 9

Margaret and I ate lunch at the deli, clam chowder and milk shakes. Helen had said in class that Margaret seemed like a person who took time to maintain her friendships. We talked about the question of having time to keep friendships alive. Some of her friendships are forty years old.

My friend, June, and I had what I thought the nearest to one that I had known. I met her in church, we taught Sunday School, ran a store, anguished over our marriages, talked on the phone, sewed, swung and gossiped on her front porch. I always felt better after being with her. She was very important to me for thirteen years, from the time that we moved to Athens until Walter left. He was jealous of our relationship at times and wished he had one that was similar. When he finally said that he was leaving I called June; she came over immediately and we went out to supper and Walter was left alone. Walter called his friend Ray, twice, before he came to be with him. June remarried the same time as our divorce and she decided to give her husband precedence over her friends. More than one of us felt the loss. I jokingly said that I had given up June, Walter and salt the same year, but it was no joke.

I discovered that Walter and I had friends as a couple, but I didn't fit into their lives as a single person. Divorce, moves and change in interests take their toll on friendships.

WISHING SOMETHING WOULD HAPPEN

Gwynne Glover Hackworth

October 5, 1981

When I look back over this book years from now, I'll think I'm desperate at this point. I guess I am. I've been more lonely than I've realized, or wanted to admit. It hasn't been easy, leaving Florida, getting married and starting a new life. My adult life. It's been real hard sometimes.

And I have to be brave. For Bob. Can't say I've done a great job—but, I have to feed his ego. No other way to put it. He does me too, I'm sure. But I have to make sure he knows I'm happy with Colorado and him. I don't think he has to do that with me. After all, it was his idea. Maybe he does, and I just don't realize it. All I know is that if I'm lonely, or homesick, I have to hide it from him, or try to. I also can't discuss with him how things are going. He wants to let them go—not look into the future. I agree to a certain extent. But I like to know where I'm going. Bob likes to get through the present until it is the future. I guess I just like to talk—not necessarily make definite plans for the future, but talk about possibilities. He gets uncomfortable.

October 9

I'm in some sort of depression. Can't figure out why. I thought maybe it was just production; I always get tense. But I haven't been real healthy either. Bob says I need exercise—my body is telling me I'm in bad shape. Maybe—anyway I don't feel at my best. Canker sores in my mouth—several right in a row and now one that won't go away—a huge one, it's been there two weeks. Also I'm getting headaches—I usually never do. And I'm bitchy.

Maybe exercise is what I need. I plan to take a Jazzercise class—but it doesn't start until November 2. I should start running I guess, but that's just not something I want to do all the time. I'd like to play racquetball, but I don't have anyone to play with.

My mind is wandering. I'm supposed to be tackling one of my trouble areas, but I'm not. I don't feel like getting into it right now. I just feel blase. I wish someone would call me or write me. I wrote all my friends last week. Maybe I'm homesick. I don't even know. Mostly I feel as if my life isn't whole. Because I have no friends, or because my work isn't the greatest. I don't know. I keep wishing something would happen, and then realizing I must make it. I would wait all my life.

I sigh a lot. Not a good sign. And I've been crying a lot too. Fighting with Bob, mostly just being a "grouch," as he says. Why am I in such despair?

I get so mad at Bob because he has no sympathy. He's a hardass—on my case and won't relent. He can't stand for me to be depressed—yet he's impossible to live with, when he is. When he's depressed, he mopes around, saying despairing things, and bugs me. I try to make him feel better. But if I'm depressed—he bitches at me, gets annoyed, tells me to stop being a baby. He seems to take it personally, as if it's his fault for not making me happy.

I just thought of sex. I never write about it because it's so hard. Embarrassing, even though no one else will read it. It's as if putting it on paper was too much. Makes it too real. It's also silly, it seems, to see passion on paper. But I'd like to be able to. I think it would help.

I don't have orgasms. There—it just looks so stupid, sounds so melodramatic. As if I want sympathy because of it. Really, I want to solve the problem. I want to have orgasms. Why don't I? Why am I cheated? Am I cheating myself, denying myself pleasure because of some unconscious reason? I can't figure it out. I've tried everything, it seems. So it must be in me. Inside my head—my body's willing, but my heart isn't. Why did I say that? Why isn't my heart willing? Sometimes I feel as if I block it. I control, I stop feeling. I know when I do this. I feel it. Like I don't want to let myself. But try as I might, concentrating, I can't help myself, I stop. It gets too much for me. I feel as though I am losing all control. Going to die. I'm afraid. I can be all caught up in it, lose control, and then just before, I stop, I pull back. And then nothing can get me there again. It is so frustrating. To Bob too. He tells me I give up. That's it—I give up. I resign myself to the fact that I can't have an orgasm, and so I don't.

I have a memory. Perhaps it has something to do with it. I remember being at my Grandad's house on Eagle Lake; I was young—three or four maybe. It was nap time. And I was in the bedroom, my uncle's old bedroom, with my cousin. I remember where the bed was—against the wall in the corner to the left of the door. I remember being in it with S. I remember, I think, him touching me, and me, him. I remember the idea of it—but not it actually happening. I can't remember if we did anything, or got caught. I don't remember sleeping or later in the day. I just remember this shadow of a memory. It's the only one I have of him.

I'd like to get past that—perhaps I'll ask my mom if something ever happened with S., if we got in trouble. After that, I remember I would never play doctor with the other kids at Grandad's. They used to play out in the old doghouse. And I would never go. Later on, I remember other shady incidents with other kids, but I would never play. I was afraid of boys up until high school—and even then it took awhile before the fear went away.

SO LONG TO GET THERE | Leslie Tompkins

July 10

    Such mixed feelings, feel ever sincere need to over-explain, go back and slow down, listen to myself, stop and feel, stop and see what I'm feeling. Don't open my mouth till I see what I feel. I wish I didn't try so hard to take a stance. Wish I could let the anger out but if anger comes out, it comes out wrong. I'm afraid it'll come out wrong like it always does . . . But I'm happy, happy, happy at school. Am I running away, escaping? But I love to get up and go out there. I love to be excited over class, excited again about something. And am I being a bad girl again? Am I being a bad mother again? How can it be so bad if it makes me feel so good? How can it be wrong or frivolous to be creative or intellectual or stimulated if it reaches that thing in me—if it reaches that thing in me I felt in college?

July 15

    Too much, too much—there is too much going on with me, in me—I jump around, jump around from one to the other. Such anger and frustration and anger. And hurt. And utter helplessness. I don't know how to respond, total loss of words, keep falling back on authoritative bitching, trying to keep control but feel like I am losing, losing, losing. Losing control, losing them, losing everything, sure and certain and calm. I am too tired to argue, to think, to respond. I am tired, tired, tired. Let me out of here. All I want to do is get away from fights and arguments and try to be rational and reasonable. I'm not rational and reasonable. I am tired and I want to leave, to get out of here, disappear, go somewhere all by myself, sleep, lie on a beach, walk and walk and walk.

November 21

    "Stop and see where the hell you are." "Get in touch with your feelings." "Get your feet planted firmly on the ground." "See where you are." What am I feeling right now? What do I feel? Where are my feelings? I can't find them. I can't seem to find them unless someone sets off anger or something. Unless someone does something to me and I am feeling nothing right now except glad I read those two books but that's not feeling that's mental and it's reassurance. Oh yes, at the store earlier, I was thinking about my friends and how in a year they will not be thinking so much about me, they will be on to other things and I'm afraid when they let go I will fall—like a child learning to walk—that knowledge (and feeling) that they are there whether I call or not. But they've been "there" for a longtime—I've been in a "crisis" for a long time—only it is reaching a climax now. I'm afraid that when it's all over everyone will expect me to pick up my life and go on and I might not be able to. I am terrified of their letting go of me, of losing that emotional support, that focused attention. It is a strain, trying to appear sane and stable and coping. Thanksgiving and Christmas will be a strain because I will have to be "happy" or at least together. It is so painful for them to see me unhappy.

WHEN MY BED IS TOO BIG   Jaki Shelton Green

i

Would you like to make love tonight
in the middle of the night
in the middle of jazz and vodka and
magic
in the middle of my bed your tongue
finds the middle of my blues
and you play each note—expertly
the way Miles plays his lips too
the way he sucks air and gives
birth to new rupturing sound
you suck air and give birth
to my tastes—oh how you play
me sometimes . . . My lips carry
the tune from your tongue
in the middle of the night
covered by our own sky.

ii

Sometimes when my bed is too big/cause/
you're not in it—i cover my head and
my nostrils remember where your mouth
lingers—remember where your manhood penis becomes full
of thunder and full of power
reaching deep inside me—my
fingers remember your skin—the
feel of your teeth sucking my breasts.

there are memories under this sheet.
when this bed is too big and i feel lost
i remember you pouring yourself down
my throat. i am a poet seduced by
sound. i make my own history.
choose my own weapons—fire my own

fires—i am a poet woman the one
you seduce—the one who makes
animal sounds in your ears—
who whimpers as you swim
lazily in her rivers.
you make this poet woman feel
like an antelope—swift—gliding your
manhood, riding you until the sun
sets. You make me feel like a serpent
coiling and coiling and coiling
around your penis, wrapping you
in my poet juices.

iii
my body loosens for you
you take my tongue out of my mouth
make me promise you foolish dreams—
you lie still beside me—the
nerves in my tongue are on fire—
my tongue traces your form—i
feel the first dew of spring sweating
inside my thighs
your hands travel—you know
this geography well—your body
has landscaped this map so many times—you have planted
so many seeds on this desert.

iv
what day is this day that you decide
to write poems for me—you place
your fingers between my teeth and
i suck your energy.
you come into me the way the
blues jumps out of B B King—you
ride me the way whales ride the
sky of the ocean and you take me
back to abandoned islands
on abandoned shore where love
and only love is the traveler.

v
you leave me shattered like rare
delicate porcelain
glistening in the sun
you step on pieces of me

broken porcelain
but my richness is fully
clothed—
i glisten in the sun—
you set me up to fall into
your dreams like some amazon
animal being stalked at dusk—
like an animal in heat
in this heat
i want to be still
to be still with you
in the shadows
celebrating sunlight and love and
you and I

vi
you could ride me tonight and just keep on
pretending that I am the A train
ride me through your south bronx
ghosts of your reckless past scream
at you much too silently
ride me tonight—i'll be your A train—
your coney island express
your cheap moment
i'll be the secret that happened
on lenox or lexington—
i'll be your junkie falling on board-
walks—but this train will come
and i won't be cold, i'll not
be crowded and i'll be bright
shadows of red blue yellow
neon, ride me, i'll be your
A train tonight, i'll give you
a lullaby you can understand
in your own language—i'll write
graffiti on your navel and plant
daffodils in your nostrils
you can ride this A train where silk
dresses caress your thighs and
feed you love from gold urns —
where agile fingers feed your
nostrils—this A train where you
want to make love to the conductor.

vii
this A train will ride you to the promised
land—wait for me there.
Stars be on fire
moon be bleeding
your wife is cold.
your wife is afraid of the sun
afraid of this moon,
this sky
these stars
she looks into your eyes—she sees
my dance choreographed before
her, a dance of celebration
a love dance
she screams
closes your eyes with her fingertips
i step outside of your eyes
dance along beside her—
she screams
does not understand why you
smile in the dark
does not understand why you
love the moon, the sea, the stars—

viii
you are a warrior who has laid
his mark on me—your mark
fell from the sun
i reach for the world
you give it to me
i work i rest i love you
i fondle the sky
you are a warrior from the
sun—your spears shoot through
me—burn me—you are riding
the promised land
        without wife
        she's gone—afraid
        to touch the sun—
afraid of this promised land
in the name of the lord
the lion of judah is my
shadow—you present me
the universe as a wedding
present—i present you pyramids

our father's land
rise up
announced the coming of our
kingdom
for we are rightful heirs to this sun -
place -
we climb to the moon
we are our fathers children first
we are sun and sky stretching out to meet each other—
we make the stars forget their
weakness and we teach them to dance—
we were never fallen warriors
only stars who had forgotten
the dance of the universe.

LAST DANCE   Wilma Wilson

June 12, 1986

    I no longer sleep through the night. I rise before the sun and sit in my dark dining room waiting for the day. I do not cry. I think, I worry, I ask myself how can this be happening?

    As I fight to understand, morning light shyly claims the room, handing shape and color back to my furniture, but bringing no answers to me. Still I sit, staring at nothing, until the muffled buzz of the alarm clock startles me, and I hear from the bedroom the stirring of the man who says he loves me but no longer wants to be my husband.

May 14, 1987

    A day to mark on my calendar! But not a red-letter day, this is a black-letter day, a day to mark with a black border and a funeral wreath.

    Phil moved out today; he finally, actually moved out. We're calling it a trial separation, but I think that's to spare distress for our children and friends. I don't see how we can save this marriage. I've done everything I could; I don't know another thing to do.

    At least the pretense is over. I'm so tired of pretending, of being the perfect couple in the eyes of everyone and all the time knowing it's a big lie—a big, fat, ugly lie. I'm so tired of all the stress and all the acting. Here I am, the girl who couldn't get a part in the junior or senior plays, and for years I've fooled everyone—even my children. But I've had a lot of practice, an awful lot.

    Now I have to learn a new role, the discarded wife, the one thing I never thought I'd be. But I suppose no one ever does, certainly not someone who went to college in the Fifties when marriage was the ticket to happily ever after.

But this is my ever after, and what I hear is silence and what I see are unfamiliar empty spaces—a blank wall where the painting from Spain hung, an empty spot where the most comfortable chair in the study sat, and half of a closet bare except for a few lonely wire hangers shoved to one side.

The children's portraits are still here, the framed pastels done as a surprise for Phil one Christmas, and the painting of Janet on her wedding day in her delicate lace gown and the necklace her father gave her for graduation. Looking at these pictures could make me cry. What will happen in six months? How do you divide your children's pictures?

So many questions. Dozens of manuals tell you how to succeed at marriage, but where do you find the rules for separation and divorce? Are there any rules?

It took thirty-two years to reach this day. How long will it take to recover?

May 15

Already I've surprised myself. I fully expected to cry myself to sleep last night, but there was not one tear. There may not be any left. After having dinner with Joan and Chuck, I came home, wrote in my journal, checked all the locks, turned off all but one lamp, went to bed, and promptly went to sleep. Morning brought the pain.

Waking up is never easy for me. There's always the struggle of forcing myself up, up, up through layers of greater and greater consciousness until finally, with great reluctance, I break through to full awareness. In this morning's battle, there was no memory of yesterday, just the familiar struggle, a few moments of unusual silence, and then the blow.

I was alone. Phil wasn't beside me, nor was he in the bathroom. There was no sound of the shower running. All was still. The other half of the sheets and blankets were as smooth as when I went to bed. He was really gone.

Yesterday, Phil left. This morning, it became a reality.

May 16

Thank goodness I did not move away as I had first planned when I saw we weren't going to be able to save this marriage. My friends are being wonderful. What would I do without them?

They have been calling all day, and others whom I know only casually have been sending messages by way of my close friends. They are determined that I will not face this crisis alone! I am amazed. The reactions of my friends were such a surprise—everyone said the same thing. After the stunned disbelief, each told me she'd known for a long time that Phil was unhappy but that she'd never once thought that our marriage was the cause of his unhappiness. I wish I could be so sure that our marriage wasn't the reason because they are all right. Phil has been very unhappy for a very long time.

Something else surprising happened. That first night, at dinner with Joan and Chuck, I actually laughed about my situation. My whole life is falling apart, the thing I most dreaded has happened, and yet, I could, and did, laugh about it. As we talked about the whole business, it seemed so unreal and absurd that we ended up laughing uncontrollably. Never in my wildest dreams would I have expected to be laughing at a time like this.

Apparently, I can no longer anticipate my feelings and reactions. The boundaries and terrain of my life have so changed that I am changing, too. It's a new role, but someone forgot to write a script. I guess I'll have to make it up as I go along.

That's why I'm keeping this journal. Writing has always clarified my thinking. When I put a pen to paper, things come out that I never knew were in me. Maybe in writing I'll find an answer I can't find any other way.

I'll record my thoughts and reactions, and maybe I'll see where I am and where I should go. Maybe I'll even see where we went wrong, somewhere, sometime.

It's only three days since Phil left, and nothing has gone as I had expected. No tears at night but a great jolt in the morning and laughing on the saddest day of my life. One reaction, however, has been a nice surprise. I resisted this separation so long because I believed, in the very depths of my being, that getting a divorce would make me the ultimate failure. Yet, as I've started to tell my friends and relatives, never once have I felt like a failure. Things aren't going the way I want, but that doesn't make me a failure, does it?

September 18

Why can I never remember?

Night erases my memory. Each morning, I have to discover again that Phil is gone. Every day is still the first day. I slowly struggle awake, reach out my hand to touch his skin, and there's only the smooth, cold sheet and the silence—silence so loud it fills the whole house and jolts me awake. There I lie, at the very edge of the bed, exactly where I fell asleep, the sheets and blankets hardly rumpled.

My mind does not remember through the night, but my body knows. It lies trapped in loneliness, knowing no matter where I move there will be no warm body—so I do not move.

I rarely woke on my side of the bed in all the years of our marriage. Phil always said if we had a bed ten feet wide, we'd use only two feet of it, the two feet on his edge of the bed. I couldn't help it. My body moved toward him as instinctively as a moth drawn to the light. Touching him was as natural, and as necessary, as breathing.

I remember the months before our wedding, how I longed to sleep with Phil. And I wasn't using "sleep with" as a code word for having sex. I really longed to sleep with him, to fall asleep in his arms and wake up in exactly the same place. I wanted to touch him all through the night. I wanted his heartbeat to be my lullaby, his embraces to shelter my dreams. I knew I would be finally home and truly safe when I could sleep with Phil all night and every night.

Where is my safety now?

October 18

Does anything hurt as much as knowing you are no longer loved? Once this man could not live without you—now he says the only way he can live is without you. Without you, without you, without you. You cannot soften or disguise it or wish it away. You were loved; now you're not loved. He might as well rent a billboard or fly a plane over-head with a banner, "You're not loved, you're not loved, you're not loved."

Does it ever stop hurting?

April 19, 1988

I remember the letters I wrote when I was in love; shy, timid letters like the shy, timid girl I was. "I love you. I'll always love you." And even later when desire and a wedding ring let me learn that I was neither shy nor timid, the words never matched the passion. Was my mind still shy or was it a passion of the body and not of the mind?

I want it again, all of it; the love, the passion, the soaring. I want a love so intense that new words must be coined to express it and new phrases woven to describe it. I want a love that envelops all the senses so each one declares its own definition of love and ever after bears the imprint of that love.

And I want the words too—a swirl of words that circle back on themselves and chase the love as the love chases the words so they spin higher and higher, faster and faster, until they topple in dizzy splendor, and the words are love and the love is words.

If I can't have it, I will imagine it.

May 19, 1991

Last night I tried to impose some order on the chaos of my writing output, several years' worth of journal entries, rough drafts, and random notes jotted on legal pads, scraps of paper and the backs of envelopes; all stacked in a tottering pile. Like an archaeologist, I dug down through the layers, finding one strata for each of the writing classes I've taken this year. The thinnest layer was from a one-day workshop last fall. Nothing was completed, just beginnings of exercises suggested to trigger new ways of looking at ourselves.

One read "Things I Will Never Be" and included just four lines:

Cheerleader.
Homecoming queen.
Sorority girl.
Guest at fiftieth wedding anniversary celebration.

When I picked up the single sheet of paper, I reread it; then, without thinking, began adding to my list:
An unwed mother.
An abused child.
A high school dropout.
A battered wife.

I slipped the page into the appropriate folder, turned to the next paper, and continued my sorting, giving no more thought to what I'd written.

Today, I suddenly realized that last night, with no prompting, no soul-searching, and no fanfare, I turned a corner. After years of seeing life in terms of what I did not have, I finally recognized the things I could have had and had been spared.

The kaleidoscope had shifted.

All the fragments of my life—the brilliant, hard-edged memories, the fuzzy, almost forgotten incidents, the dark-colored opaque hurts—had always tumbled together in my consciousness, but no matter how I adjusted my vision, it was always the same few frustrations that fell to the center. There they lodged, magnified in the mirrors of my mind, reflecting their images back and forth, until I could see nothing else.

Time and experience kept shaking the pieces, creating ever-changing arrangements, but the same worrisome pattern always prevailed. Then yesterday, the old bits fell aside, long-forgotten nuggets suddenly caught the light and a new design emerged, sparkling with precise clarity and affirmation.

How or why it happened I cannot say. Maybe years of therapy finally forged a new connection, maybe my writing prompted a new focus, maybe an old pain somehow lost its grip, or maybe—just maybe—I'm growing up at last.

May 24

A man I met last week at the singles' meeting called to ask if he can take me dancing. I panicked, but promised to call him when I'm back in town.

"Go," my daughter says, "you keep saying how much you've missed dancing."

"Go," my new friend Dot says, "you like dancing, don't you?"

"Oh, yes," I exclaim, and I tell her my dancing history, a history that began, like so much of my life, with Phil Wilson.

I tell her about high school, and how we danced at the Rec after every football game, and every basketball game, and every Friday night in between. And about the wonderful summers when we could dance several nights a week, not just on Fridays and Saturdays. And those special times, the junior-senior proms, the Rainbow Girls' Christmas dances, and those rare trips to the Blue Moon, a bona-fide night club in Springfield, where we danced to live music far into the night.

We never danced to fast songs—Phil was not comfortable with those—but we rarely sat out a slow one. And, oh, how we danced, dips and twirls, and back and forth, across the floor in bold, sweeping configurations. No small, tight circles in one spot for us. Phil's brother refused to dance for years because he thought he could never compare to us.

We danced less often during college days, but around the memory of those dances a glow remains even now. This was dancing fueled by love. This was love ignited by dancing.

Then we married and moved back and forth across the country from one Marine base to another, then north to Michigan to design school. Out of school with two children and only a starting salary, we had little chance to dance.

Years later, when we happily settled in the South, dances came back into our life. But dancing didn't.

We went to dances, but now we sat at a table most of the evening except for two or three very special songs when Phil dutifully whirled me across the floor. What had been a delight had now become a chore for my husband.

"I never stopped loving it," I tell my new friend, "but, for the last several years of my marriage, we rarely ever danced."

I replay these words in my mind, and I suddenly see it isn't true. Phil and I didn't stop dancing, we just changed the steps.

There was no music playing and no one said, "thank you," at the end, but we were dancing, an intricate *pas-de-deux* more significant than any two-step we ever guided across the floor. Only now, Phil held out his hand and beckoned me to step smoothly aside just as I approached. Then as he lifted his arms about me pantomiming an embrace, I tossed my head, slipped under his arm, and glided away.

Back to back, we teased each other, taking one step forward and two steps back; and, as our lips moved to one tune, our bodies moved to another rhythm. When I reached out to pull him to me, it was he who turned away. So again, we twirled and dipped, but never touched, never in unison; we moved in ever-widening circles until the distance was too great to cross, and the music no one heard ceased to play. Like all dances, this one, too, ended; but I didn't go home with the man who brought me.

This was our last dance—a dance choreographed by anger—the final chapter in our dance history.

LIVING FROM DAY TO DAY   Rita Berman

The first indication that anything was wrong came when we were staying at the beach in July 1981. We were spending a week at Emerald Isle before Jessica was to start college. She had brought along her boyfriend, Joel, and I was hoping that the romance would not prevent her from sticking to her educational plans. Apart from that, everything appeared under control. Our lives were proceeding in an ordinary fashion, not necessarily dull or boring but in that familiar, pleasant routine that comes after many years of marriage. So it was that summer, the lazy days at the beach and simple pleasures, no real worries.

In the early morning, while the air was still cool, and before the sun warmed the sand so that one's feet felt scorched, I would take a walk before breakfast with Ezra or Rebecca. Walking along the beach, stooping every now and then to pick up a shell, we'd talk a little, and watch the gulls and sandpipers feed at the water's edge.

Some days Ezra fished at the edge of the surf. He's fair-skinned and has a tendency to burn rather than tan, when exposed to sun. He hadn't learned to slaver himself with sun-screens and hide under long-sleeved shirts and long pants. About half-way through the week, some red, blotchy patches appeared on his hands and he showed them to me. It must be the salt spray, he said. I noticed the blotches also were on his back and shoulders. One of the moles appeared larger and redder than I remembered, and I suggested that he show it to the doctor when he went for his next physical. He gets a complete medical check-up every year and was scheduled to have one a few weeks later.

For the rest of the week, he stayed out of the sun during the hottest part of the day. We went sightseeing to Fort Macon and the quaint town of Beaufort, with its Mariner's Museum and well-preserved clapboard houses.

By the time we returned home, most of the blotchiness on Ezra's hands and body had gone. A couple of weeks later, when he had his physical examination, the doctor said he didn't like the look of the reddened mole. He suggested that Ezra have a biopsy taken to see if it was skin cancer. It all sounded very routine, just another test.

A week or so later, the biopsy was done. Ezra got the results a few days later. That night, with both of us sitting in front of the television in our recreation room, he told me very calmly that it had been confirmed as a malignant melanoma.

Melanoma. The word shrieked in my mind. A quickly spreading tumor. At that moment, with Ezra talking so calmly about something that was shocking and frightening, it seemed unreal. This can't be bad, there's no music, I said. Without music to guide us, unlike the dramatic scenes in movies or on television, we don't know when something bad is happening.

But even without music, the scenario played on. Ezra's next step was to discuss the report with the proper authorities at work and to make arrangements for the necessary surgery and treatment. Schedules must be consulted and appointments made, nothing happens overnight. So he carried on with his work, and I with mine.

They say that illness ranks high on the list of stresses. The first Friday in September was particularly trying for both of us. In the morning, we were scheduled to meet a leading cancer specialist at Duke University Hospital, to discuss the details of Ezra's forthcoming surgery. And that same afternoon, we were booked to return to the same hospital to the Eye Department so that I could obtain a second opinion about retinal holes, which were increasing in number and size. We both behaved calmly but were scrambling to cope with the big "C" and the possible loss of my eyesight, if one of those holes reached the stage of detachment.

The plastic surgeon described the operation and the type of scar that would be left on Ezra's mid-back. "I'll excise the melanoma and close the wound with a rotation advancement flap," he said. This ended up being a scar similar in appearance to a question mark without the serif. He informed us that radiation or chemotherapy might be required, depending upon the severity of the tumor, but we wouldn't know for certain until after the operation.

The operation was scheduled for the following week. During all this time of tests and discussions, Ezra had appeared to be almost off-hand about his situation. His attitude was one of let's get it over with. Fortunately he wasn't in any pain and couldn't see the mole, so he did not appear frightened. On the other hand, I was very emotional about the situation. I felt frightened and vulnerable. I couldn't face dealing with my eye problems, so delayed the treatment my doctor had recommended. My anxieties lay with Ezra and the unknown. I would wake up at night and look at him sleeping by my side and wonder if he would be there next year. Awful thoughts to cope with. During the day, I could push them aside by occupying myself with the household chores, or researching a writing project, but at night there was no place to hide from my fears.

Rebecca and I went to the hospital the day after Ezra's operation. On entering the hospital room, we saw Ezra sitting up in bed wearing what struck me as the silliest-looking hospital gown. It was patterned all over with yellow and blue ducks and I thought, how utterly ridiculous, why was he wearing a gown made for a child?

He had a drip line in his arm and looked rather woozy but was very talkative, almost garrulous. What he said seemed so out of character it startled me. For the first time in many weeks, my matter-of-fact husband was expressing concern about his condition. It was as if, after undergoing the operation, he finally realized, or felt he could voice, the seriousness of the situation.

I'm at risk, he said.

I know that, I said, I've been worried about it for weeks. But how come you weren't until now?

He explained that the night before the operation, he had been visited by a psychiatrist who worked with the oncology department and specialized in helping cancer patients understand their illness. No one before had talked to him so revealingly about the statistical probabilities and possible consequences of his illness, he said. As the psychiatrist talked to him, he realized they were working with real numbers based on lots and lots of data. Faced with this type of information, it finally occurred to him that the chances they were talking about related to him. Conversations with the other doctors had focused on describing the tests, and what methods of treatment could be used, but no one had talked about what it meant to him as the patient in terms of the rest of his life. The night before his operation, he finally understood there might not be much time left.

Rebecca stood quietly listening to all of this but I could see her eyes grow round and her face lose color, and I knew she was deeply troubled. Her father, who rarely expressed himself in an emotional manner, was letting on that he was very worried.

Within a few days, he was home to recuperate, and then we were given the good news that the tumor had been completely excised. It had not penetrated the muscle layer so chemotherapy treatment was not required. His back was covered with a large dressing that made sleeping uncomfortable but, by the time this "backpack" and the sutures were removed, most of the discomfort was gone. His recovery progressed and aside from times when he felt a sensation of pulling, as if there wasn't enough skin to cover his back and his range of motion was limited, it was uneventful. He went back to work and to his pragmatic attitude.

Ezra appeared to recover physically and mentally from his bout with cancer and was able to return to his former way of life of taking each day as it comes, but it had a profound effect on me. In the early days of his post-op recovery, I felt like I was walking on eggs; everything had to be approached gingerly. And for months after the operation, I listened with heightened anxiety to the slightest comment he made about feeling tired. As he went about his business confidently and calmly, it was I who still needed reassurance that all was well. My fear progressed until I called the Cancer "Hot Line" at Duke Hospital. They were helpful in telling me what signals to look for, in case he had a recurrence. At night, when he undressed for bed, I would surreptitiously check his back to see if there were any changes in other moles. Eventually, enough time passed that I could anticipate the future in a positive way.

May 16, 1991

In February, when I called our friends and relatives to tell them that Ezra was undergoing tests and might have lung cancer, their reactions surprised me.

My sister-in-law got angry with me and, in later phone calls, owned up as to how she had always disliked me. I now wonder if that was her way of rejecting the terrible news.

My sister, who lives several thousand miles away, murmured vague platitudes. "It will all turn out for the best. Having cancer could enhance the quality of your lives," she offered. "It gives you time to plan."

What a ridiculous idea, I thought. I can't imagine how Ezra's cancer is going to enhance my life. Ann went on to describe the funeral she had recently attended where the woman had chosen the music she wanted, the kind of service, and so on, so that her husband knew exactly what to do when she died. That phone call was no comfort.

I wasn't thinking of planning Ezra's funeral yet. We had only been given a tentative diagnosis by his family doctor and he was scheduled to see a pulmonary specialist at the end of the week.

I spoke calmly to the others but, in reality, I was worried. The sound of his cough fell like a sharp blow on my ears, reminding me that he was ill.

Earlier in the week, I had tried to escape from the cough by taking all of my winter shoes down into the garage and polishing them. Even with the door closed and the radio turned on, the sharp barking noise intruded, I couldn't block it out.

At night, it was worse because he disturbed my sleep with his coughing, twisting and turning. Sometimes I had to finish the night sleeping on the living room couch.

Some people fell silent when I told them Ezra's news. I learned to wait patiently while they digested it. Then they asked questions, mostly the same ones. "How did he find out?" "When did it happen?" Do you think it was his smoking that did it?" After a few such calls, I had my responses down pat. I told them how it had started with a bad cough he had in January. As for the smoking, well, it could be; his doctor wouldn't speculate on how he got it, only that the X-ray and CAT scan showed a mass, and his symptoms indicated cancer. In order to be certain, he has to go through something called staging.

The advice came freely. "Join a support group," said someone. "It will help you get the anger out." What anger, I wondered? I couldn't tell what my feelings were. Some people told me about their own cancers, of which I had previously been ignorant, and I felt saddened because I had no comfort to give them.

I continued to go to work, maintaining the cheerful attitude that everyone expected. Get-well cards and letters arrived in the mail along with books and articles on how to conquer cancer. Ezra wouldn't read anything about cancer, so I read them for him.

At night, I stuffed myself with chocolates while watching television. Five minutes after turning it off, I couldn't remember what I had seen. I felt bone tired with the strain of it all.

I do remember sitting in Duke Cancer Clinic's waiting room, waiting for Ezra to see a specialist. A soap opera was in progress, the type of program that I dislike, but I sat there watching the characters furrow their brows and tighten their lips as they emoted pain and suffering in an exaggerated manner. In real life, everyone behaves calmly, no one at the clinic looked like they were suffering.

May 20

Ezra has been very ill and is still undergoing chemotherapy for lung cancer. He is halfway through his treatments. It was on Valentine's Day that he got the diagnosis, after having a CAT scan. We have all been on an emotional roller coaster since then.

First hoping for an operation, then learning it was too far spread in the chest, and the only thing that could kill the cancer was chemotherapy. He spent three weeks at Walter Reed Hospital after suffering a near fatal reaction to the anesthetic used in the bronchoscopy. Too much administered.

Now, he is adapting to a new regime, three days a month of going to Duke, working the rest of the time, but not very energetic. . .

Jessica is here with us, and Callie. Callie is time-consuming in her needs although she is a happy, good-tempered child. She is a toddler, sixteen months and ready to explore her world. We all love her, and she brings such lightness and joy to us.

November 14

Ezra has completed all of the chemotherapy and six weeks of radiation, and now it is only a matter of check-ups that keep him seeing the doctors at Duke Hospital.

The latest prognosis is he has a sixty-five percent chance of surviving two years; the longer he goes without a reappearance of the cancer, the more chance he has been cured. This is not one of those five-year survival situations.

I have felt drained, or numbed, during the past months. Even our trips to Andros, Nassau, and Vancouver did not stimulate me to the point where I could forget that Ezra is ill, that there is this terrible shadow hanging over him, and me, and that there is nothing we can do about it. He looks better, his hair is growing again, he is cheerful, but nonetheless I feel that shadow.

June 22, 1992

I have been in a "throwing out" mood this past week, going through some old letters I came across from Ann, written over the years. In particular, a lovely note from June 1959 on my twenty-seventh birthday. The tone was so optimistic for my future and expressive of love to me as a sister and friend that I couldn't throw it away. It was also revealing for pointing out how I have allowed myself to get dragged down by life. Where is my sense of humor these days? Where is the fun, the impromptu happenings, the excitement of perhaps meeting a stranger who will open up new worlds, or a job in which I can receive the recognition I deserve?

I'm mentally and emotionally floundering, and Ezra thinks it's because either I haven't gotten over not having the girls at home and haven't found my purpose in life, or else it's because I am receiving little encouragement in the way of publication of my writing.

I don't know if it is as simple as that, although the girls did take up so many years that I had to put myself on hold, so to speak. And then, too, Ezra's job took us to some dull towns where there wasn't much opportunity for new, exciting things to happen. Also, even within the framework of a long-term, reasonably well-adjusted marriage like ours, I feel that I have had to make the greater adjustments and have had to alter and slow down my expectations to those of Ezra. Perhaps it is that which scares me, as I don't see him becoming more dynamic. He is content to live from day to day, and I usually look forward (or back).

My writing, well, yes, I haven't found an editor or publisher who cares for my fiction enough to want to publish it. And as for the non-fiction I'm bored with business stories, so I can't go back to where I know there is a market. I have written a couple of stories on our trips to Paris and England, and they are circulating.

No, I think it has a lot to do with reaching the age of sixty and thinking, "What now?" And knowing that, in another few months, Ezra will be home full time, and then what? I booked a week at the beach for us in October and, apart from that, Ezra plans to work on his models, sit and read, and do a little volunteer work. Some of his attitude may be attributed to his normal behavior, and some may be linked to his cancer and that he is waiting for the two years to pass before tackling anything new. At least he has progressed to talking about a possible trip to Portugal next spring.

Someone told me once that the reason people get paid for holding down a job is that no one would do it unless they got paid for it. Some jobs, paid or not, are just that onerous, uncalled for, back-breaking, mind-draining, boring and life-depleting. A few make us feel as if we'd like to pay for the privilege of doing the work. But most work is somewhere in between.

We Southerners have this thing about work that goes beyond the bread and the bacon and the pate it puts on the table, that it has intrinsic worth. We maintain that it builds character and keeps us out of trouble, this notion a residue from distorted Puritan dogma that said if you were tired enough, you wouldn't get into trouble. And if you didn't get into trouble, that you could work more. Generations of mischief-making has proved this wrong. In fact, today there is probably more mischief on a Friday night after a hard week's work than our ancestors could have shaken their work-worn fingers at.

What kind of work then, is "love made visible?" Much of our work as Southern women is to try to answer this question. We have never been strangers to work despite the stereotyped pale, ruffly, fluffy, china doll who hung on the arm of husband or Daddy, coy, helpless and manipulative. Most Southern women would have liked a little pampering and a few ruffles. We have butchered hogs, dressed the dead, nursed the sick and wounded, delivered babies and buried them, managed boarding houses, driven trucks, slung hash and rivets, shelled and canned enough green beans on a wood stove to trace the path of the Great Wall of China. We specialize in doing what needs doing and write in spite of it.

Journals of women are filled with this same adamant spirit toward work that their grandmothers directed toward spiritual discipline in their pious journals. In our writing, we try to separate the truth from the fiction about work, to understand the difference between the work we choose and the work that chooses us. Many have exchanged the Augean stables of housework and field work, the factory and the mill with its withering routine and physical hazards, for the psychic hazards of the board room, the shop, the office and the academic committee. We have traded the legacy of work left by our ancestors and hope to escape the treadmill, yet wonder on Friday nights if we have not just swapped one mill for the other.

PHASING OUT   Stella C. Cook

December 18, 1990

It is getting harder and harder for me to do my job. My heart is not in it. I know my job will end on June thirtieth, so any incentive I might have had has been sifted away through the phasing out of my job. My "get-up-and-go" has gotten up and gone. Anything I do requires large doses of energy, even the simplest of tasks. I resent investing anything of myself in the work, now that I am so close to leaving. My emotions are mixed. I am glad to leave, yet I am sad to leave. I will not miss the repetitive routine that I have settled into as I go about doing my work each day. Unfortunately, in this field of basic protein chemistry research, you are at your best when you can repeat your work in the most precise detailed manner. The only true variables in the experiments should be what you designate as variables. Any change in the results should be attributed to the changing variable, not a variation in technique. The repetitiveness of the work allows you to get a clear look at one change at a time, but if you have just an ounce of human emotion, it drives you to distraction, as you shut out your personal thoughts daily, in order to carry out the precise details of the work.

I have learned some rather complicated work since I've been in this job, and some of my experiments are so complex that it takes a week to run one from start to finish. In some cases, had I not written down, in advance, the protocol of my project, I would not be capable of interpreting the final results, simply because I could no longer remember just what the experiment was about, after the days had passed.

This work has stretched my mind to do some unusual procedures. I find it stimulates me to write compulsively. I have no outlets emotionally in my work, so I funnel it into my writing. It will be interesting to see how my next position feeds the writer in me.

January 4, 1992

My experience in the lab leads me to believe there are no careers that are not tainted with discrimination or prejudice. Since I have been in science as a technical professional, I can only speak with authority regarding just that one narrow area. It was mighty naive of me to think that I could slip into science and side-step the preoccupation of keeping the black woman in her place or, shall I say, the socio-economic levels properly separated. I do believe that this racial preoccupation is not racial at all. It is that black people are just now getting into some fields, and so we have no political clout and carry such high profiles that it is not considered proper to condone us yet, much less do favors for us. What appears to be racial is actually political. What is done is usually done because it is politically sound, not because it is the right thing to do. It is just that we have been treated so unfairly for so long, we no longer concern ourselves with what is the norm. We simply want what we feel we should have gotten years ago. The politics does not concern us, but it does concern society at large, and so, if we intend to beat the game, we have to play politics, to a certain extent. Generally we gain entrance in a vocational arena, in the beginning, by being simply extraordinary. This is how white society feels we pay our dues. They gain entrance by playing up to each other. Black people can do that if they happen to know some-one, but usually when a field has few blacks in it, we know no one so this other approach of being extraordinary is more realistic. I have worked in clinical labs and basic research labs. For clinical labs, a medical technology degree with a pathology certification is required, but I managed to get into a clinical laboratory through the blood bank and hematology by carrying my one year of graduate school around high enough on my shoulders so that everyone could see it. In one hospital, they let me into the blood bank with the understanding that I would take one week of training, when the normal training period was three weeks; mind you, this was with a white friend on the inside vouching for me. Once I was actually on the job, I was told that absolutely no mistakes would be tolerated. I didn't make any mistakes. That is what it took for me to enter the nearly lily-white lab without rocking the boat. Because of my extraordinary accomplishment, they eventually went from two to one person on the night shift in this lab, with a person on call. I cross-matched blood with no checker, and people who worked in my place did the same.

In basic research, the story has been the same. Almost all of the work I have done has been novel, yet none of the scientists under whom I worked felt any urgency to give me credit for what I had done. I have seen credit given routinely to white men with no degrees in labs in which I worked, even though they were doing straightforward, uncom-plicated work, which had been laid out step-by-step for them by the principal scientist under whom they worked. In my case, I was generally given very difficult projects which had not been worked out, requiring repeated exposure to harmful chemicals and, when the work was done, I was given credit as a technical expert when I should have been listed as one of the authors, at the very least, since I was the main driving force behind the project. The white males I knew could be replaced by another technician, and similar results would be obtained. A Ph. D. with unique experience would be required to supply my expertise, and even then similar results could not be assured.

I have decided that I will probably never receive credit for what I have done or what I will do in the future in laboratories, so to secure the future for my children, I must obtain higher pay. That will not make up for the lack of respect for my talent, but will certainly make me feel better about myself. More pay will make me less sensitive to this matter and help spur me on to becoming an excellent writer.

My goal is to be gone from my present job right when my boss leaves next summer. At the end of January, when the head of the department tells me that he is phasing out my position, I intend to ask him to write me a letter of termination so that human resources can get started on finding me another position.

If I end up with no job at all, for a while I will work with a local company that specializes in placing lab personnel on temporary jobs. I may be able to get a permanent job through them. This is a nice compromise for a person like me who knows no one in a position to help me get into a lab in another company. I know people, but none of them are politically sound enough to speak for me so that I can get a job based on their word.

The head man here seems to be trying to learn what I do and get what he needs done before I am gone. I will not go unless I get a job that pays me as much as, or more than, I make now.

Already I have decided my approach on my new higher-paying position. I will do my work and only talk to other people when it helps my writing or my job. My personal life will stay just that, personal. Since my marriage ended, I have wanted another job. I want to start everything fresh, everything new. A new job will give me a chance to start over again. Phasing out my job is forcing me to move in that direction. I welcome the challenge.

MY SMALL PART OF THE WORLD   Robin Greene

July 22, 1991

I write now, only a couple of weeks into living in our new home. I must say that I surprise myself by enjoying it. Although it's awfully suburban and conventional, it suits us. The baby is negotiating the stairs well—no need for a baby gate; and Dan seems to love his new, large room, which is over the garage, the last room down the hall, and therefore a bit removed from the other bedrooms. There is finally enough space to fit us all, and all of our belongings. And with space comes, hopefully, organization and peace of mind. When my external environment is chaotic, I begin to feel out of control and find that I lack the peace of mind to think and write clearly. Does this process belong to women only, I wonder? Michael surely doesn't seem to have this same need for external order.

I turn my attention these days toward my writing. Winning the chapbook contest this spring certainly has given me confidence in myself. And I'm amazed at how much the world's influence and opinion affects me. I no longer feel like such an idiot working in such a solitary, solipsistic way. No longer do I feel so isolated and out of touch.

Always when I write, I write to please some imagined, highly-critical yet intelligent and well-read individual—a perfect reader. When my poems come back rejected, I sometimes feel that my reader wasn't on this particular magazine's staff, and that my poems just weren't good enough. The small success of winning this chapbook contest has given me a sense that if I keep striving (regardless of rejections), sooner or later I'll get there.

July 23

It never ceases to surprise me—I always feel good after writing. This evening, Michael took the kids out for an hour and I was able to work. Sometimes I feel that writing is the only thing that sustains me. Although I know that this is not really true, I love my crazy and demanding family, and would feel very lonely without them. Why then is connectedness so important? Are we programmed biologically to need others? To need to procreate, to need to nurture, to love a human being in more than just a sexual way? And are my needs as a woman different than a man's needs? I know these questions have been asked over and over, but they still interest me.

July 24

After a non-productive day—one which began at 8:00 a.m. with a trip to the pediatrician for Ben—I sit here at the computer and look over two uncompleted poems, first drafts, at best. Ben has another ear infection and is once again on antibiotics. Who knows how long he will sleep tonight? A depressing thought. This getting up night after night really takes its toll on me. I feel too old to mother such a young child—though many of my peers have young children. My kids are older, in fact, than some, especially Dan, who'll be ten in September. I wish sometimes that we had had another baby closer in age to Dan—then both kids would be relatively independent by now. At one-and-a-half, Ben is difficult. But regardless of how much he wears me down and taxes my strength, I love this child dearly.

Outside, I hear thunder. From my desk I can see out the window to watch sheet lightening momentarily brighten the night sky. To add to the drama, the tall pines are beginning to sway, and I can hear the breeze blowing through the needles and leaves. Now a swift crack, and the rain begins. I can't look at my poems, which seem like failures, my failures. I can only do what I can do, I tell myself. And Ben's wakeful nights can't go on forever. How incredibly difficult life is. And how unprepared I am for it, although to judge me from the outside I'm sure most would agree that I seem to be managing. After all, I have an M. A., an M. F. A., a book of poems coming out. I'm a college teacher, wife, mother with two thriving kids. But even after parading all this out in front of myself, I still remain unimpressed. In fact, my feelings of desperation, depression seem to be intensifying. Maybe I'd better leave off writing for now and read a book.

July 27

I want to try to articulate to myself why writing is so very vital to me . . . why I can't give it up, though I've had relatively little success. And why, I ask, have I had so little success—lack of talent, lack of perseverance, other goals that subvert my attention? And I don't want to tell myself what I already know: that I write because writing is a long-standing habit, and it is a way by which I define myself.

I began writing when I was in the second grade. I have a clear memory of sitting in the finished basement, the playroom, at the round table, underneath the dim hanging light, and composing my first creative piece, a short story entitled, "Monty the Dog." We had recently bought a puppy and I had been out-voted in my desire to call our new dog Monty—a name I found both handsome and suggestive. The name seemed princely, noble, seemed to possess the ability to connect our family to something better than it really was. Names were magic. I remember wanting to change my own name at many different moments during my childhood and adolescence. And I did finally adopt a nickname, when I went to college—and enjoyed what I thought then to be a new identity to go along with it. The name "Monty" was short for "Montgomery"—again, a most beautiful and prestigious-sounding name. And when my parents and brother decided on "Gidilah"—which is Yiddish for "big deal" (because we had been making such a big deal over our new pet), I decided that I needed to "have" the name that I liked so very much anyway. So I took control—the only way I knew how: with words. I wrote my story and played out the fantasy on a couple of lined sheets of white paper. I scrawled out the life that Monty, Montgomery afforded me. I don't remember the story's plot, or if I saved the story or even showed it to anybody, but I do remember that during the writing of the story I felt at peace with myself. I felt as though my imagination—both spiritual and intellectual—was at one with my sense of self.

July 29

This idea of writing as a way of taking control over the world seems important to me right now. (Perhaps because I feel so out of control.) I know that, as children, we are, for the most part, powerless, so it makes sense that writing or creative expression would be a positive way for kids to manipulate their world. Children learn how to become powerful and effective by learning how to manipulate ideas and people. Maybe when I began this journal with the idea that "I write because I'm in the habit of writing," what I was really saying is that I write because I'm in the habit of manipulating my small part of the world with words, as a way to feel more in control.

I have one memory that has always stayed with me—has seemed intrinsically connected to my sense of myself as a writer. It was parents' visiting day at my sleep-away camp. I must have been nine years old. I was very excited as I sat on a wooden swing located on a rise from which I could view the entrance drive to the camp. I looked forward to seeing my parents. And they were bringing with them a big yellow stuffed elephant that I missed and had asked for. Also, I felt that I had grown up a lot (I had been away for a month—the camp was two months long), and wanted to share this more mature self with my parents, especially my mom. I was swinging higher and higher, as I watched the entrance road for our familiar family car. But I never spotted it. Then I saw two strange adults walking up the hillside toward me. They were smiling and carrying a large yellow object. Still I didn't recognize them. I just kept swinging. Then they called out, "Robin, Robin!" But I kept on swinging, somehow still not realizing who they were. At the very top of the rise, my eyes lighted on the object the strangers carried and thought, "That's my elephant; these people are my parents." I jumped off the swing to greet them, feeling off-balance and vaguely ashamed. All my happy excitement had vanished. My parents hugged me and offered the stuffed elephant, which didn't look like my elephant at all. But I acted the part I felt I was supposed to play. I kissed them, hugged them and walked off with them hand-in-hand to show them my cabin and introduce them to my camp counselor. That night, after they left, I remember feeling that although I inhabited my body, the real, the inner me, lived somewhere else. I pictured my brain as a round, grey cavern, and the person I felt myself to be lived inside that cavern— small, shapeless, invisible to everyone, yet somehow very powerful at the same time. I was frightened by my thoughts. And frightened by the thought that my parents could so easily be separate from me, that perhaps I no longer needed them like I had as a young child. In fact, I sensed that I already needed to further my separation from them and live as an individual. All these thoughts and feelings came to me without understanding. I certainly loved and needed my parents, and yet, I felt guilty and disloyal, as though, in my mind, I had already betrayed them.

July 30

It's interesting to me that, as I read over some of my entries, I'm realizing that I'm writing this journal, these words, as if to a stranger or strangers . . . as though, once again, I'm swinging on a rise, but this time the people walking toward me whom I fail to recognize are really parts of myself with whom I need to speak, need to explain. Is this what the impulse to write might be: a kind of self-talk to the strangers within oneself?

HONEYSUCKLE VINES AND KUDZU   Betsy Blair

October 1983

Tonight I don't know what dance and choreography are. I wonder why I have spent so much time moving . . . was I dancing? What have all the hours been about? I am suddenly tired of the piece I'm working on and want to finish it up, get some response and get on with it. How self-taught I have been and certainly that has brought me deep into my own way of dancing and teaching and moving—but I've missed the expansiveness of knowing about other ways of dancing. I feel something of an amateur for not having had "formal" training and master teachers.

I have always wanted to be a dancer, even when I was very young, but it seemed such an unattainable and such a difficult and such a ONE-track path. I went for multiplicity—and in the sixties who would have even thought of dancing as a way of "helping the poor, etc."? In the seventies who would have felt like a liberated woman in trying to make a living as a dancer? I really did an admirable job—considering.

Dancing and making my body spirit glow for others and sharing my intuitions and feelings may be the best things I have to give to the world. In a way, it really doesn't matter if I'm trained or not, the really important thing is that I continue. Even when I don't feel that I'll ever really be a dancer or that I'll ever really be trained to be a dancer. The fact is—I dance, I make dances. I teach others how to make dances.

Every day I am involved in one way or another in this passion. It is what I labor at on this earth. Dances are what I form out of the energy, the space and personalities that float about me. It doesn't matter if I really don't know what I'm doing—so there!

But, my God, what if I am a dancer? What responsibilities does that entail? So I get my body ready, so I gather up a group of dancers. So I produce works, so I costume them—so what, if they aren't marketed? So what, if there's no place for viewing them, so what, if there's no manager, public relations person, true believer to package and sell! So no one sees, so no one cares—unless I (little red hen) make it happen.

The true test of my self-assurance is going to be in the marketing of myself as an artist (regardless of whether I feel like I'm one, a real trained one or not). It doesn't really matter. I always have and always will be well received, regardless of how I feel about it in the grand scheme of the unattainable "real" dance.

I am not fake, at least. I've got too many hours and performances under me to be a fake. So I'm not a great master. I'm just a local dancer who makes up dances all the time—more than anyone else around, that's for sure!

It's all in the attitude

and my attitude is always going
to be dedicated
            disciplined
            discriminating
                    and
            damn self-assured
This is what
I have to learn!
This will be
the difference in
making or breaking.

CRITICAL BELLE   Janis Butler Holm

Writing—a strange phenomenon. I want to recover the kind of self-confidence I had as a child—what I wrote was good because I wrote it. I've since internalized a nasty critic, one who slaps my hand before I've put pen to paper. Who is this censor?

Me: Who are you, critic?

Critic: I'm many people: mother, father, teacher, preacher—everyone in your life who has represented standards.

Me: But all of those people have wanted me to accomplish things—they haven't tried to block me, as you do.

Critic: I'm also a part of you that wants to punish you.

Me: Yes, that's what I've suspected. But where exactly do you come from?

Critic: (Silence)

Me: I'm going to find out—the point of this journal is to guide you to a more creative, productive role. I'm tired of your tyranny.

February 16

The problem: how to find one's own rhythm, when rhythm seems to be no more than the beats and pauses of others.

The solution: to listen to oneself.

I want to write. Who is stopping me?

Myself.

Such a wide gap between the sophistication of my understanding and the clumsiness of my expression. When I read this much later, will I equate these poor, empty little sentences with my feelings at the time? (Shut up, Critic.)

May 29

In alliance with The Critic: The Belle. Part of me thinks I should be sitting over a silver teapot on some Texas ranch. I'm gonna get that bitch!

October 23

Why can't I put pen to paper in reasonable fashion? What is going on inside? What is the irrational resistance? COME OUT, whatever you are.

What is in the way? Have I been denying myself the kind of nurturing I need? When I was younger, I spent all of my time with books, fantasies, insulating myself with other people's worlds, and that insulation allowed me to write. Have I since turned my back on something important? Have I denied myself escapes? Have I temporarily lost a crucial thread—a strange bond between myself and the world of words? Have I tried to become someone other than who I am?

November 11

(Somewhat angry with myself when I read this journal—all of the ritual and repetition concerning writing, all of this talking myself into it.)

The Critical Self—this very destructive critical faculty that— still—works against my best interests. This Critic must be exorcised.

December 4

Fantasy: an academic journal entirely devoted to the subject of my particular kind of writer's block. Title? Critical Belle.

| ALIEN IN THE KITCHEN | Betty Hodges |

February 16, 1968

I rush to hang up the clothes before the court trial for last night's demonstrators and lose the joy of outdoors. But it is satisfying to get them out, housewifely.

At the courtroom the place is still rickety and black faces line the walls. An impatient bailiff runs everybody out but those seated and makes some spectators get up to permit witnesses a place. He lets me stay when I tell him I am there from the radio station, but I am uncomfortable.

I am relieved that the cases are postponed, but back at the paper I am still excited, stimulated and scrabble about, listening to Chuck and Mac speculate about what will happen tonight and tell of the pictures the Herald did not run.

Home, my instant lunch and a walk before settling down to the review of "Gone with the Wind" the other night.

Afterwards, I look out the window to see my clothes flapping nicely on the line. It is satisfying.

August 21

We break another record today with a 98. In Fayetteville, it is 102, the weather report says. I do two survey interviews, one in the morning and one in the afternoon, Louis puttering with his models before the fan in his room; Mely with me.

By four I take them to Duke Park Pool, guilt-stricken over neglecting them to work. It is so hot I get in the water too and it helps. The little black children, in their ill-fitting suits splash each other in the shifting battle of survival. The lifeguard's whistle blows constantly to stop the rough tussles. It is different, not the skin, no, but the behavior pattern. This culture merging, or whatever, will take some doing on the lower middle class level, the only one where any mass contact between the races is taking place; and it unwilling.

September 26

The children and I roar in the VW Bus over to Chapel Hill after school to hear Joyce Crawford talk about her book at a library tea.

The cookies go fast, with Joyce's six, my two, several of Dorothy Mullen's and three of the Graces. Joyce's five-year-old still has the soft baby look that is no more in this house.

"I always wanted to write," she relates, "but there was never 'time'. . . . I realize now I didn't want to bad enough at that time, or I would have found the time." Listen, Betty.

October 31

I take the drip pans out of the stove to scrub. Grandma comes this weekend. I leave them to soak in soapy water and when I go to make the beds the burner coils, all standing up on their hinges, make the stove look like a spider, after me, I know.

November 23

I come up out of the cauldron of work that is the Parade of Homes assignment to turn again to writers. It is delirium to sit and read of M. De Jong, to search his ideas on the work of the subconscious in the creative process, as the rain encloses the house and me and the world and Louis' Calico sleeps with one paw over her eye to keep out my light.

March 6

The hum of my dishwasher is a cozy thing as it robots a whole day's eating and cooking utensils clean while I pound away happily at my typewriter. I sometimes turn to embrace its warm bulk in gratitude.

March 24

I despair under the burden of three survey jobs at once. The house lies dormant under an accumulation of tracked-in dirt and risen dust. The sewing machine beckons to me sadly and I cry helplessly at the seeming hopelessness of it all. Time, time, time, where, when?

March 25

I sit under the hair dryer and read the Ladies' Home Journal: "Dr. Donald MacKinnon, an authority on the 'creative' personality, has kind words about inferior housekeepers. They are more apt to be creative: 'A creative person admits to disorder in his life. He likes the richness of it. He is seeking some farther-reaching quality of order.'"

I grasp at straws, but am heartened.

May 9

With three full hours, I profligate in the files of the North Carolina Room. I take all of Phillips Russell's clippings to a quiet carrel and ebb and flow in the cocoon of it. Is it only the contrast to the business of surveys and people and the clutter of the house, or is it inherently this sweet to be so alone, so left alone?

May 20

A bright booklet of decorating ideas comes in the mail addressed to "The Homemaker at 1613 Hollywood Street." I cringe. Is there one here?

May 27

I admire the top-stitching on my mu-mu—it marches steadily and evenly over the yoke, neatly unlike the frazzling bother of all the things that nag at me.

July 8

With Ed and Louis at Pope Air Force Base overnight, Mely and I make short shrift of breakfast. I am through breakfast, beds and dishes easily in time to trundle off to Hillsborough on a garden column. On the way I feel the sense of order, the "being-about-it-ness" that is the antithesis to the feet-in-quicksand feeling I have on the mornings I stay home, trudging clumsily through chores.

In Hillsborough, the horticulturist at the county agent's office takes me in his Volvo about the country to talk to gardeners who raise vegetables to sell on a "pick-your-own" basis.

A Mrs. Mincey, buxom and damp from her bath, returns happily to the corn field with us, picking me a dozen ears of sweet white corn, loading me down with tomatoes and cucumbers and inviting me to pick all the snap beans I like from the loaded vines climbing the six-foot corn stalks.

In the red mud of the rows, I doff my sandals and lose myself among the big leaves. I am a child again, newly arrived in the Model A with Mama, Grandma and the others at wart-faced old Mr. Sayre's truck farm to buy green beans and tomatoes for canning, corn for supper and cucumbers for pickling.

Faced with Mrs. Mincey's bounty, I feel an earlier awe of such an abundance of ripening vegetables, staggered by the work they represent, the rich plenty and the contrast with the stacked, shipped shelves at the grocery store.

At home, I slice cucumbers and onions together, cook the tiny peas and strip the shucks from the corn for a supper we all eat like famished hikers just back from days lost in the woods. It is another kind of eating than from cans, another kind of nourishment.

August 4

It rains incessantly. There is water standing in the basement of the addition, the clothes pile up for want of drying and unseen mold creeps over everything. Little seems possible at all.

November 5

Folding towels from the dryer, I am an Orphan Annie, carrying stacks of folded clothes from room to room in whatever house she is established at the moment. All those rooms, all those stacks and she endures. Will I?

February 17, 1970

Liz Tuehling is efficient at her desk, while I interview her husband on the bird course he is teaching this spring. As we talk, she works on a list of bird bandings, turning her records of thousands of birds caught, marked and released, into neat figures for the Department of Interior's Fish and Wildlife Service. I marvel at the order, the clarity she has created from all those different moments she spent, mornings, afternoons, when with a sparrow here, a towhee there, gone now, where? North for the spring. And I despair that ever the birds of my life caught in unintentional nets, will become in my hands, neat rows like that.

LET THE AIR SPEAK MY NAME | Jacklyn Potter

February 27

I come back, I come back from the flatlands, the mountains, to the Tidewater of Virginia. I live in no particular moment. No family. Nothing. I am the universal woman, generalist to a default, speeding, racing, writing all poems, reading all poems, sewing all clothes, dancing all dances, taking all jobs, reading all books, indeed writing all books, following all roads, drinking coffee and falling in love with all women, a glimpse, like a round crevice in Magritte's sky, tells me what the true ego experiences.

March 16

I must write on the first day of my new job. I am so nervous but I believe I'm going to truly have a job where I do all the things I know so well to do, and I'll get the credit for once in my life.

March 19

I dig the earth and get paid to do it. I am an Extension Agent. Taking soil samples. Now that's a new title. I am astonished at this change in my life. I must get up early and walk and write. My boss is blue-eyed, pleasing and southern. My heart soars, the crocuses pry from the earth, the birds are talking again. I drive past all these fields, many greens, it's my job!

I danced for two nights at the Pines, and I know I love it! I am certainly happy. The local Chincoteague standers, who just stand every day at the corner: Taterbug, Frog, Tadpole, Catbird. I visited Ruth, who slipped and broke her hip on the ice. She said, Jackie, some people are suited for each other. You need someone to talk to. You want to have a conversation with someone. You can't go through life all by yourself. These masses, they think differently from me. It's just another level.

April 25

I got to work early, and Pete gave me seeds for 4-H kids' gardens. Jo Anne and Bob, my island friends, and I plant our garden, and Bob thought of using whirlygigs—little windmills. To scare critters.

April 26

It's a gaggle of geese I see. Seven. No more. Job continues to amaze me. So relaxed. Yet so interesting. It's raining now so hard that the drops bounce back up, silver ball bearings, waves on the causeway. I live in the extremity of nature.

May 1

I love my job. It seems it's going to end in August. Gene says he is going to try to get me a job. I am going to do an amazing job with 4-H, and I am going to insist on staying. There is so little development of 4-H clubs here. Pete is not exactly interested in kids.

And I won a first prize for the first time in my life, the Paul Ernst First Prize in Poetry from Salisbury State.

May 6

I am so depressed, fearful, that my job may not continue. Tomorrow I will speak to Cary T. about this job. He's Gene's boss. Maybe he can help with some specific guidelines.

May 15

Virginia people have qualities here I admire, and I see them with their ways, quiet, slow moving, utterly helpful and showing their feelings. They don't judge without empathy. And Gene has the great sense of fairness that goes deep, deep, saying "ever so long." Using "whatever," ever being a mainstay of Virginia language here.

June 1

Here I am being a woman in my new apartment. I am so in love with life. Let it never be said that I don't conquer those dreadful pains that cause despair. Pete tells us he's leaving Extension. I am sad he's going. It certainly was nice being with a regular guy, a farmer who loves plants, fields and bees. He even gave me some bees, so I could have honey all the time. Horticulture, not kids for Pete.

June 11

Where is the ego? Is it in the left toe? In the cuticle? It surpasses the soul in importance. I am on the beach. It is perfect.

June 16

And the job! It suddenly terrifies me. I am unable to fathom all the work I have to do. And what guarantee that it is mine! Even though Pete leaves.

Tomorrow I'm filling my flower presses and then I'm going to the beach to tan my hide. Wild flowers pressed for summer camp. For the bookend craft project I am designing.

June 26

Am I really an Extension Agent? Or am I a writer/poet? Being an agent has a charm but see how little I get done of my creative life! All I do is drink coffee. And plan, look for volunteers and meet many wonderful children.

August 3

The kids call me, saying, Ms. Jackie, we grew a big cucumber; it's getting real big, but it don't taste so good! Later, I take them a recipe for zucchini bread, laughing out loud in my car.

August 9

Today I did well, in spite of getting up late. Tangier Island! What a trip! Did well with twenty-three kids. They are blond, proud on Tangier. It's a mystery. Tangier. I watch them. Who could know what goes on in their minds? Who could? Friendly. Certain about day to day. No cars. Only bicycles. I ride past the mayor!

August 11

Today, a momentous interview! I am going to be interviewed for the job. The permanent job, left by my Pete. Do I want it? I really can't lose. After all, I have been trained. But if not, I'll be a CETA extension agent. Gene always says "you can do it." All the evidence still not in. Today among nine others for the job! I wonder. Do they dare refuse me? And still, I don't know where I belong.

August 17

I am so amazed at this portrait: I dance, eat, sleep, glance, dance. I write boring memos. And boring number reports about the blacks and whites I contact! Abe! Martin Luther King! What do you think of it all coming down to this! (But don't put the black kids in the clubs with the white kids . . .) These new multi-racial clubs really have an extra dimension. No kids object! So I put 'em together.

September 10

I don't know how to write this. I lost the job. I am not going to have the job. My life is utterly bleeding. I am wasted, wanting—I need a light, I need brute lust to show life. Can I deliver peace and joy to myself, lacking others? At least I have Gene's support. He was so upset and talked with me. He urged me to talk to Supervisors who vote on the appointment. The Blacksburg Deans chose some other guy. Gene is so angry.

Let the air speak my name, claim my stillness. Can I be? Am I a brightness apart from that burning? What pose do I know now? These are not rhetorical questions. Let me down into stillness. I am prepared for a new death in life, known as stillness. *I Ching* saying "fire always needs a source for burning." When I throw the coins, the hexagram is Difficulty at the Beginning; "It furthers one to appoint helpers."

September 15

I write in here, now that my life has run out of boundaries. Consciousness a thread of fear trailing through my being, my very fiber. I carry on. I fear now Gene speaks against me. I don't want to do battle with him.

September 16

Shatters, the shatters are the loblolly needles falling around me, the shatters are not the needles, but the sound of the needles as they come down to the ground, so sandy, seabound, seawise. The shatters—the sound of my life breaking past me, the sight of my life, thinly held by the slim hand of a man who will not help me. Has it always been thought that men are crucified? Was it Jesus, the man, on the cross? It must be seen how women hang too, that women hang there, in great sorrow, and worse, surrounded by indifference.

EACH DAY AT THE EDGE   Nancy Simpson

April 14, 1982, The Golden Isles

Here I am, back in Brunswick and The Golden Isles of the Georgia Coast, the same glorious land I was in this time last spring. I am on Easter break, visiting in the home of Doris Smith. By now, I am convinced there is no better place to be in the springtime. It is perfect beach weather, and I have spent the last three days beach bumming alone on Saint Simons Island. Doris goes on with her writing as if I were not here. Still, we have large amounts of time for talking and for going places.

This evening, I am trying to take stock of my own situation. I am relaxed, slightly burned, and I feel sort of sad for some reason. I have had three days all to myself, lying in the sand, with the sound of the waves lulling me into oblivion. I feel close to myself, as if I have almost reached home. Parts of Brunswick, especially Old Town, remind me of Miami, Florida, when I was a girl growing up there, and I have been flooded with old memories. Driving through the wooded areas of Saint Simons Island made me think I was back on Key Biscayne, located just off the Miami mainland, where I used to swim and picnic as a child. That is where I spent Senior Skip Day with my friends, there at Crandon Park, when I was seventeen. What I am enjoying most about this trip to the coast is running each day at the edge of the surf, like when I was a girl, my lungs bursting, yes, and my mind dazzled by the brilliance of reflected light. By now I am feeling good, and a little daft.

I hope the sadness I feel is a sign that a poem is emerging. I have not had a poem in a long time, as you know. The critical work in the M.F.A. Program and my everyday rush-rush life is not conducive to the writing of poetry. Somehow, I have to get beyond the creative block. This is, of course, the major reason I came to the ocean. I am absorbing a tremendous amount of energy on the beach, just sitting in the sun, and I would like to believe I am regenerating old energy into new by running. I want to convert all the energy now into creative energy. What do you think, Buddy? I think mega-energy will hit me sometime tomorrow, halfway between the ocean and the mountains. If the energy converts the way I imagine it will, there will be no other way to spend it in a cramped car except to spend it as creative energy—which means—a poem, a poem—I hope.

You want to know what I have been doing for the past three months, why there are not more pages filled. I have been teaching special education classes, as usual. I have been a mother, a daughter, a sister. I have been studying modern and contemporary poetry with my instructor, Heather McHugh, and have been seeing a few special people now and then, and writing large numbers of letters to correspondents. Every day, without exception, I pick up my poetry folder and make a revision or two. In all this, if a new poem starts to speak in my imagination, I drop whatever I am doing and write. By now I have learned to drop anything for a poem.

The M.F.A. semester is only half over, but Heather has indicated that she is pleased with the progress I am making with the critical prose. Maybe I will be fit to do the degree-year essay next semester. It looks certain that I will be studying with Ellen Voigt, since I had a note from her saying, among other things, that I should send her a copy of all my annotations and my ideas for the "study topic" so we can "hit the deck running."

One major development in my writing life that pleases me beyond words is that State Street Press is going to publish a small collection of my work in the form of a chapbook. Judith Kitchen, my newfound friend in the writing program who took my manuscript home with her from the last residency, turned out to be the editor of State Street Press. What good fortune for me!

And the most encouraging thing about my overall work is that both Heather McHugh and Judith Kitchen believe my manuscript is complete and it should be making the rounds of the publishers. I know I don't have a snowball's chance, but it is exciting to have the say-so of these two women. Judith has the manuscript still, and she is putting the poems in order for me. She has a gift for that sort of thing. I am re-typing the individual poems now, with the latest changes. I feel if I do not get it out of my sight soon, I will whittle the poems down to nothing. You know I would rather revise than eat.

A RAMSHACKLE BOARDING HOUSE CALLED TIME

Becke Roughton

December 4

I've done it again—burned dinner. I stepped in the studio just to get something, when a line of a poem I was working on earlier pulled me to the desk chair with the gravitational force of a black hole—noose is more like it, a crime against womanhood. Phew. Burned again. How will I ever be a real live certified woman if I don't take more interest in cooking? How will I ever be a real live certified woman if I don't wear jewels and wobble on seven-inch heels into an immaculate dining room while extending my fine china hand and long perfect nails—and darling everyone to death? How's that for fiction. March to a different drummer. Sure, but nobody ever said what that drum might be made of.

December 5

Thou shalt love life more than the meaning of life— Dostoyevsky. Spent the last four days going around the studio cleaning up, out, round about. There is not really much more room in here but it feels different. I threw out bags full of poems. The last time I purged the kingdom was several years ago, when I threw away over five hundred drawings. It wasn't done in anger or disgust (those are the times not to throw away), but because it had to be done. It feels like fluffing up a feather mattress, then diving into it, though the process is the reverse— contraction in order to expand. Challenge yourself. Take risks. Motion through faith.

December 6

Time is a distortion. I'm still working on the large painting, still coming up for air and always the shock of what the surface looks like.

Sometimes I would like to prefer talking about my work more, then I could bubble on and on about this and that. One time at Yaddo the comment was made that there would be no lack of conversation with all the writers present, who proceeded to talk non-stop through dinner and on into the late evening. It must be the artist in me that comes out. I'd rather put the energy into the work itself and talk about other things. Or not talk at all. Someone once said to me that it must be wonderful to both paint and write. Sometimes it is. When your fingers get tired of scribbling in the cramped space between the elbows, you can spread out and work on a large painting or drawing or hammer some wood together. But the most frustrating thing is that there is not enough time to do all that I want to do. To push both disciplines as far as I want them to go. I know the best approach is to enjoy both and do what I can, as I can. It is not writing and painting as a career, but as a necessity. I can write and then go run to break the rhythm or pace, but running doesn't take that long, especially since I'm not training to become a long distance runner, or reach California the slow way. No, sometimes doing writing and painting is a curse. They are very jealous lovers, these two. They live in a ramshackle boardinghouse called time. And the rent is always going up.

December 15, Studio Time.

   Must be about 5 p.m. by the way the light has blurred the pines across the street. And by how dark it is in here, though I've lit the candles—a ritual carried out every day in December, no matter what. I hear the cats fighting like the animals they pretend they aren't. That is a sure sign it is 5 p.m. And then there will be dinner to burn again for the humans.

December 16

   The large painting progresses laterally. It's insane to try to work with canvas dimensions over a few feet in this little closet. Then I think of the other absurdities—Pearlstein working in the corner of a room no larger than this. And Giacometti during the period when months of work could fit into a matchbox, those figures that kept diminishing.
   Working on smaller studies of portions of the painting, to work out the problems. It's also interesting to see which parts can develop separately to stand alone.
   The constructions are personal—like a scrapbook—but of other lives. They take a long time—arrange, rearrange—like playing chess—waiting for just the right move, the right object, not something you can make always. The constructions are more related to collecting. What is painting then—trading—between myself and the canvas? It certainly has a control of its own some days, no matter how much technical direction I give it. With a brush in each hand, I enter the tent. A white rabbit carries a glass box of colors. He slings a black cape across his other arm—asks if I believe in magic.

December 17

   Yesterday there were over a dozen mourning doves pecking on the trampled, cold clover beneath the feeder. Usually I see only three or four of them at a time.
   Winter—when the trees become etched against the slate sky. Well, that's how I'd like it and forget about the warmish, brilliantly sunny Carolina blue skies—at least when I am drawing. Every branch exposed at last—those charcoal lines, intricate, irregular—the peach, dogwood, the dotted possum haw—some trees like lace, others craggy enough to growl at you. From the studio, if I stretch to one side, I can see

the sun set through a cluster of tall branches across the street. On some days, it is so stunning I stand perfectly still, watching until the sky becomes a purple bruise, then the light sort of flickers out like a candle. It is as if the earth, or even my body, has absorbed all the colors. It's actually more restful to watch this than to go out running, though I don't like to admit it.

A MOUNTAIN ALL AFIRE | Lorraine Hutchins

December 3, 1976
　　Yesterday the Black Caucus presented their demands—exciting, angry, scary, fascinating—a big goddamn relief! They're right to be insulted that we would go talk to the old black citizens on S Street, whom we need zoning approval from, without taking them. And that the new board members being nominated are too white.

December 10
　　Yesterday we did an incredible amount of thinking and planning work together—about long-term fund raising, salary levels, Christmas and the kids. And meetings with the Mayor's Advisory Board and the Carter Transition Team. We agreed to quit the end of the year, if we can't raise $10,000 in salaries for each of us.

January 4, 1977
　　Still want to design the New Year's letter and scare up other new funding leads. Plus smack Runaway House into shape. Where does the anger come from? I think partly from the Black Caucus—how full of boasting vision and demands they were in December, how little they have to show for it except raggedy shit, now. And yet my expectations of them suddenly becoming competent managers or at least decent warriors, does that have a racist tinge—honky wanting good black role models to debunk her stereotypes too?
　　Our sense of community is tenuous and wounded. I want the richness back, more than ever, still.

January 6
　　Jay, Mary, D, B, Jim and I met with Otis and Barbara about the state of Runaway House and where to pull it from here. A difficult meeting, but glad I was there. Every day it gets harder to know if we'll succeed—but my energy, enthusiasm, compassion for the kids doesn't cease.

January 12

Today trying to pilot a ship that's mostly mutinying. Facilitated meeting where Runaway House was outrageous, threatening, flinging around their wounded shit. Betty said she could almost walk out the door and quit, set up an alternate corporation, take the (more white) group foster homes with her.

January 20

Yesterday's meeting most exhausting one so far. But there was more concern there cradling us, less willingness on the part of the whole group to endure interminable jive. We met huddled in our coats and gloves in the Runaway House dining room, because of the broken furnace we can't afford to fix. Sat in that same room where it started eight years ago, talked about closing down, said we couldn't work together, was it worth saving, how?

January 26

Melissa quit yesterday. Dear, white, remaining Melissa. The scary impulse is in me too, in all of us white folks, in some way, I suspect—the vengeful, exasperated, "OK, take it, take the program you've fought and railed against, it's yours." Similar to what all colonizers indulge in as they leave, leave their mess for the others to clean up.

January 27

I know I came to that meeting with a vengeance yesterday, the same way I see them enter Runaway House with gloved fist and then admit later that their own lack of that open hand slapped them fully back, met resistance at what they sought to do. What good does it do to punish the new black counselors, rather than figure out how to train them? We're all caught in roles we play out at the expense of our common growth.

I want someone to grieve safely with. The tremendous pain and sorrow I feel when Dennis says there's no challenge left for him with "those people," that he sees them as "infantile," is "embarrassed" to raise money for them. Yet I accept, from his lonely position, how true it is, how little he trusts now, how much he needs to be shown.

January 30

"Roots" rocks the nation, everyone talking. The changes at the houses are visceral. More hostile, but also more proud.

March 9

I am stunned. This may be the end. Dennis and I talked of closing down by June; he and Betty have decided to leave, marry, start a family of their own, give up.

April 23

I really believe in my vision, my faith in the organization, making a difference.

Spent six hours this afternoon at Runaway House doing the collating and labelling with them. Being at Runaway House with the kids, their agitated, whimsical energy, was good for me. Very healing. Tiny came by with her baby. Was very pleased I printed her poem.

MOTION ONLY I CAN SEE

The diary/journal is a patchwork quilt, a self-pieced piecing. Like the quilt, it's a matter of time that emerges through writing and the meaning the writer finds in it, from outworn tradition, myth, innocences, expectations, injustices, dependencies, dark times, barren times, silences, and sweet momentary joys. She buys time by giving her parturition with no birthing a name. A journal marks time by moments in the story that the writer is telling. The journal is a map of where she has been, a range finder for where she is going. It is a daily log recording the terrain where self discovery can take place.

And yet giving birth to yourself is not always that hard or that serious. It's just that we Southern women have much to cast off, and much to lose if the ballast is cast overboard. Deciding what to scuttle takes time, and writing helps. Questions of direction, decisions, crossroads and bypasses, we try them out and ask "What if?" And through the journal pages, we express the authentic self which does not need to be disguised. And sometimes we try on hats, like I used to do in my mother's closet, for just plain fun. Is it part of that urge of adolescence, to peer in mirrors, check what is there? Perhaps that is what is meant by "becoming."

ALONG THE PATHS, A KNOWING | Maggie Wynne

See, in the center is Maggie—a single red rose. Hold it close and see the tender unfolding that cannot be forced. Breathe deep the fragrance that it gives. The fragrance is deep red—like the color. Though you take one breath and another and another, in each breath you find a different sweetness. Is that a lemon fragrance? Is that a hint of gardenia that's seeped in? The fragrance that I give is not a simple one, but it is ME—an essence that is mine.

In soft profusion 'round the rose are lilacs in lavender, deep purple-reds, and here and there a few branches of the rare white that is so lacy—so fragile. Lilacs that surround me are nostalgia, sweet memory, tender beauty and sad truth of lives that have nurtured mine and continue to. Lilacs are Ama, they are Mother, they are Great Gama, they are Aunt Susan. They are Virginia—bittersweet place of rooting and coming forth. A place where women held on—held to life and insisted on beauty. Women who would again and again settle for and accept and endure—but one thing they would not live deprived of— beauty. The beauty of loving and being loved. The beauty of creating a place in the midst of what they could not control or understand. A place to be—a place to receive and to give—a place to say, "Here I am."

Scattered among the lilacs are the wild flowers I have gathered. Here, wild daisies, not the huge, showy florist variety, but the simple, dainty, real daisy that shoots up on a slender stem with such courage to say, "Look, see me!" And there is a delicate Queen Anne's Lace and here and there are nameless wild flowers I cannot put a name to. I cannot say whether I have gathered them or they have gathered me, yet along the paths, across the fields and meadows, there was a recognition, a knowing.

BURNING TIME | Stella C. Cook

October 1, 1991

I enjoy going out in my yard and clearing away the debris which the trees have made. Now that it is fall, there is quite a mess outside. The leaves I automatically rake each time I make a pile to burn, but because there are so many beautiful trees on this land, which are in various stages of growing up, maturing, and dying, I often find myself clearing away pieces of wood as well. Sometimes the pieces of wood I find beneath the trees are rather small. They appear to be something the trees have discarded because they are no longer needed. Other pieces have been quite large and required the use of handsaw, ax and wedge. These devices were required to make the pieces of wood smaller, so that I could move them to my designated place for burning. A couple of weeks ago, I found the entire trunk of a dead tree out in the front of my lot in the graded clearing beyond the trees, near the dirt road. That thing was quite a job for me to get up, with no chain saw. I started my project by first clearing away all the broken limbs which I could carry with no sawing to be done. Then I started manually sawing on the trunk itself. I had only sawed away the top section, and the project had gone from one to three days long, when the entire trunk disappeared. I think my next door neighbor had something to do with this dead tree leaving so quickly. It had fallen so that it was on both of our lots, yet it originated from my lot. He might have felt that my method of disposing of the trunk was somewhat slow, or he might have felt it was preventing me from cutting the grass out front completely. I often cut a small section of his grass when I cut my own out front, so that everything looks uniformly manicured.

This year, I did not have a traditional garden plot. I used the fluffy soil made from the ashes of various places where I had burned brush, dead wood and leaves to make three nice flower beds. This past summer, I filled those beds with corn, tomatoes, peas, turnips, okra and green beans. Next summer, they will actually have flowers in them, and my newer beds made from brush piles I am burning now and will burn between now and next summer will accommodate my vegetables. I intend to plant butter beans, peas, tomatoes, okra, corn, melons and cucumbers.

My mind has about as much emotional debris as some of the trees in my yard. The debris comes from problems which I take on that I can barely handle.

Right now, I am trying to send a boy to college. This is his first year, so I am learning of the expenses as he goes. Fortunately, he worked this summer and managed to secure scholarship money to help himself. He still needs my financial backing and emotional support, though. This is quite an adventure since he is seventeen years old.

My daughter is still very much alive and has her affairs that I take part in also, so I have to divide my time and energy between the two of them. With so much to do regarding my two children, there is little energy to do for myself. That is my problem. I need to work things so that I manage to get something of myself expressed in my life, also. Writing a journal has been my regular but erratic way of expressing myself in the past. It is no longer enough.

I need to do more of what I want to do, and less of what I need to do. The trick is to design my life to accommodate such a thing. I know that I will not become independently wealthy in the near future, so I must set into motion a rational plan to work this problem out.

A good place to start, I think, will be with small blocks of time each day. Just the way I burned small pieces of debris from the trees in my yard and got so much enjoyment, I will start to burn small blocks of my time in my life and learn to experience the same enjoyment. I may start with lunch with a co-worker at first, or maybe even a movie with a friend. I will continue to write each day, intentionally taking more and more time as I do. My writing used to be for pleasure, but now I have come to depend on it to release my pent-up frustrations, and so I must write longer periods of time to reach a point where I am writing for pleasure. My sewing hobby will again be resurrected along with my birding, which I intend to teach my girl also. Just as I accompany her to music lessons and practice with her, she may find it interesting to learn to sew with me and watch birds, to the point that she can name every local species.

Learning to burn time for my own personal reasons will not be easy, but in order for me to grow as an individual, it must be done. It is just as important for me to do what needs to be done as it is for me to do what I want done.

June 3, 1991

Can my writing release me from the daily grind of routine, everyday work? Am I clever enough to make pen and paper work for me? Yes, this is something within my capabilities. It'll take time, but I can. I will give myself seven years to churn up a writing career, more time if necessary.

My mother called last night. I sent my parents a very happy postcard so they called instead of writing.

I've made up my mind. I want to become a writer, and from now on, that's where my mental energy goes, into my kids and my writing. I am no longer pursuing relationships with people, that simply does not work for me. I have finally learned to be content within myself. People have taught me that over a period of time. I feel isolated from them, even when I am in a crowd. I don't really understand why, but I do know that there is a wall between me and them. I wonder if our life experiences separate us from one another. Maybe I want that wall, and for me, it signifies protection.

Writing is my ticket to freedom. It's going to break me out of my social cell block. It's gong to unlock my stopped-up mind. Writing is going to bring my life around.

What I like most about writing is the requirement to be alone to execute it. This is one profession, other than research, where time alone is required in doing the work. Unlike science, writing requires some public contact, otherwise how would you know if what you write would get read, or is being read?

How is it that sometimes when I'm talking, I hear the voice of the person who is not speaking? His silence punctuates the sentences I say. His eyes and facial expression interfere with my freedom to think. Why do his words, unsaid, have such a powerful impact on the words I am speaking? Why do I know so well this unspoken language? This language is like the unsung parts of a song surrounded by singing. It takes the silence in music to accentuate the melody. The silent language of my listener defines whatever I say. This language, known by babies, children, adults and even animals, is sometimes a more powerful means of communication than words.

WHAT SHOULD I BE DOING?   Gwynne Glover Hackworth

November 1, 1981

I'm afraid of blind faith. Whatever happened to make me not trust? Why can't I have faith? Nobody's ever let me down—except myself. Am I so ashamed of myself? What have I done that's so bad? What haven't I done? Why have I no faith in myself, and so can't trust others?

I am a good person, I think. I am kind, and good, usually, basically. I care about other people. I'm not mean. I love other people.

I am smart, and fairly wise. I see things, I understand. And I use my brain, my smarts. I know what's going on in the world, and I care.

I am ambitious, and hard working. I want to be involved. I am involved. I have a career, some goals, some purpose. A direction. I have a good job, using my god-given talents—and I do my best at it.

I am attractive, pretty even. Not beautiful but good looking. I am fairly sexy, could be more, though. I am gracious when I need to be—am well spoken, have good manners, dress well.

So why am I not satisfied? That's how I can classify myself—not satisfied, unfulfilled, unsure.

I am unsure of my looks—so unimportant in the larger view— but obviously important to me. Why? I am not ugly, far from it. We place such a high value on looks. I am not satisfied with my ambitions—don't feel as though I am doing what I should be doing. What should I be doing? What am I not doing?

The answer doesn't come to me. I know I am a writer. That much I know. And I know I write well. No longer unsure of that. It has to do with what I should be doing with my talents—brains and a penchant for words. If I'm not doing something good, and being recognized for it, I feel as though I'm worthless. I must be good, no, the best, at what I do. I'm thinking of my life—first, school and grades, Girl Scouts, softball, all sports, cheer leading, student government, journalism, committees, awards.

I was the best in all of it. And now nothing. My problem is not adjusting, though. I still feel I have to be great, not that I just need to get used to not being great. I am driven by some inner voice—always hammering at me. Coaxing me, scolding me. Nothing less than greatness will be accepted.

AND SO DIRECT MY LIFE Eleanor Roland

Judy says we must find time to write every day. So here I am at work, trying to write a line or two. With work and all my other commitments (the choir, sorority activities, the Commission on Women, etc.), I can see why I have no time to write. I must begin to eliminate some things from my life. I find if I turn off the television, I can quieten my thoughts and get something written down. I can also understand why black women in the past have not had time to write. There has simply been no time "for such foolishness."

Last week ended on a good note. I planned and made food for a cookout for my daughter, Leslie, who just started graduate school at Duke, and her M.B.A. classmates. It turned out to be quite nice. I did get annoyed that my husband decided to play golf rather than stay around to be of help. I decided, however, not to let his unavailability bother me too much. I went on with the things I had to do. I had planned my day rather well, so the question was one of timing and carrying out the tasks I had to do. Organizing one's day and writing things down help a lot. Leslie and I had planned the menu and what each of us would do that day. She spent the night with me, studying, while I rambled about in the kitchen, locating pots and pans that I use only once a year, now that the children are gone. I only cook big meals about twice a year. At the end of the evening, about 9:30 p.m., I finally sat down and reflected how much I had enjoyed the day and meeting Leslie's new friends. The cookout had gone well. The students hung around for a long time afterward. That let me know that they felt comfortable at our place. It brought a lot of joy to my life to be able to focus on doing something for someone else. I still must talk to my husband about his lack of participation.

October 10 (later)

Today is Friday and the end of a very hectic week, both on the local and national scene. I am ready for the weekend. I am in need of a vacation, really! I've worked a whole year now, which includes finishing the dissertation, adjusting to a new job, and now with trying to lose weight, singing in the choir and going to meetings, I've overdone it. Our financial situation, as well as mother's health, also wears me down. I have not walked in two days and I think that is also part of the stress I feel right now.

My husband and I have begun to talk a bit about the money situation and his disappearing acts. Regardless of how bad it is, I think I do feel better when we put stuff "on the table." I call it "saying it out loud." Let each of us hear each other, and perhaps some solutions can be worked out.

Anyway, all of this stuff is on my mind, yet when I go for my daily walk, I find the time to breathe in the clean fresh air, bask in the blue sky, and really feel at one with God. I do feel better, too. I find myself watching the little beetles and bugs, crickets, grasshoppers go about their work regardless of what else is going on around them. Does not God care about me as much as he cares about them? I believe he does, and I think I will be helped through the rough spots. One cannot enjoy the sunshine unless one experiences the rain. That, I suppose, is an axiom of life. I am a survivor, and I will survive. I think the writing helps make it all come together, too.

October 22

I'm doing pretty well. This is the second night in a row I've taken time to write. Today could be summed up as a great day. The weather was beautiful—an Indian summer day with the right amount of crispness in the air. Indeed, the last days of summer. That is one of the joys of living in the South now. The leaves are slowly showing off their rich fall colors. We had rain last week for two consecutive days and, although the temperature dropped, it seemed to be just what was needed to enrich the array of fall colors in the cluster of trees. Before this rain, the leaves are slowly turning, but the colors seemed dull browns and burgundies. Now I see more brilliant red, yellow and orange leaves. I do love fall and spring. Though the two are opposites, one representing a renewal and the other a fading away, they are, for me, the two loveliest times of the year. Perhaps there's a message in that revelation for me. Find time for renewal! Perhaps I should so direct my life.

TAKING THE HINT   Vicki Posey

I'm in my new office. Actually, it's not just mine; I share it with three other adjuncts. But I'm the only one who uses it, I think. I really like it that way. It's in the music annex, next to the gym, and I like that, too. I usually hear people practicing piano or whatever. The office is not great—musty smelling, a bulletin board covered with decorative foil across one wall, cheap curtains on another (I really don't know why). I am sitting on the only chair that is high enough for an adult; the rest are small, as if meant for preschoolers. I keep planning to bring some things in—a lamp, coffee maker, but so far I haven't. The job seems so temporary that I wonder if I should bother.

I'm just beginning to feel normal again after an awful bout with a virus and bronchitis. I was literally in bed all weekend, the weekend before last. I had the worst chills and fever I can ever remember. All weekend, I just wanted to curl up in the bed and stay warm. I felt like a cocoon and remember the feeling of my breath coming out of my mouth, so hot that it almost burned my hand. I was hot, but wanted to stay hot and really couldn't stay warm enough.

I love being here now, writing, looking out the window, listening to the quiet. Sometimes I wonder what I'm doing here and feel like I can't teach at all. But I think it's good for me to struggle with it.

October 14, 1991

I read yesterday about a woman who lives most of her life in a cave. She has friends but mostly lives there alone, cooking and making do all by herself. Sometimes I think I'd like that kind of life, at least for awhile. Living in a cave appeals to me very much.

When I was growing up, my life at home revolved around work and activity, involved little associated with books. My father read the newspaper, *Mechanix Illustrated*, and the Bible. My older sister read comic books. Other than these, we had a dictionary—torn and scribbled on—and a set of *World Book Encyclopedia.* Our town had no city library, no bookmobile and, in the summers, even the school libraries were closed. I don't remember having stories read to me as a child. So, in essence, I had to learn how to read books. They were like puzzles to me. I wondered what all the fuss was. I'd heard that reading good books was important, and I wanted to know about it. But, at that time, I just could not understand lots of it. That summer, I finally gave up on *Raise High the Roof Beams, Carpenters* and read *Gone with the Wind*. Although it took me all summer to finish this book, I did understand the story and this gave me great hope for future reading.

I now feel that buying *Raise High the Roof Beams, Carpenters* was an extremely important event in my life. As a frugal teenager, working in a dime store for five dollars a day, I debated whether I should buy a magazine for fifty cents. Why did I buy this strange book that I knew nothing about for the huge price of seventy-five cents? Now I'm sure it was one of those things that was meant to be. The book is still one of my all-time favorites. I don't remember exactly when I read it and felt I understood it. I do know that on first reading, and for many readings thereafter, I had no idea what Salinger was referring to when he mentioned, on the second page, a "Taoist tale." Only much later did I learn that this Tao or Zen philosophy permeates much, if not all, of Salinger's work. I love the fact that the first book I ever owned begins with a Taoist tale. I've read the book dozens of times now. In depressions, I use it to make me laugh. When I feel good, I read it for sheer pleasure. To me, it's one of the funniest and saddest books I've ever read.

In other areas of my life, I fell into activities with Zen ideas, too. When Lee mentioned how much she liked the violin she saw on "Sesame Street," I investigated Suzuki violin lessons for her. I had heard about a program that taught very young children to play the violin, and I thought it was worth a try. When we started the lessons, I really had no idea what we were in for. I just thought of Suzuki as a method of learning music. Now I know that it is much more, and that at its center are Zen ideas.

It's funny how things in life add up, how in looking back, we can see patterns. Throughout my life, I've written quotes that I later learned were from Zen writers, many from the *Tao Te Ching*. When I first read this book, I was awed. Other works as diverse as Joseph Campbell's *Power of Myth* and Betty Edward's *Drawing on the Right Side of the Brain* have been very influential in my life, and these, too, contain many elements of the Zen philosophy. Jung once said something like, "When life gives you a hint, take it." I think life has given me a hint.

I am sitting in John's room and writing and looking out the window. It feels so good, like this is something I should be doing. I don't want to go anywhere else. I get so unfocused at times and think I should do this and that—teach aerobics, take a real estate course. If I can remember to be still and write, I will be OK. Stillness is something I love but I have had little of. I remember, as a child, being so rushed, so busy at our house, so that sometimes, when I had spare time, I either didn't know what to do or felt guilty, if I didn't want to do anything. As I write this, I know, in a way, this is not entirely true. I remember wonderful times, sitting in the cottonwood tree or lying in the grass, doing absolutely nothing. But, in actuality, I think these times were few and far between. Maybe that's why I remember them with such fondness. Stillness. I will be still.

TIRED OF WAITING   Sue Lile Inman

1983

A message of liberation for us captives has come to me from Alice Walker's *The Color Purple*. I have the urge to copy out the whole section of dialogue between the marvelous character Shug and the protagonist Celie when they are discussing God, and the crippling image of God as the white old man that so readily comes to mind, especially devastating to the black person. Shug's concept of God deserves to be read and re-read.

What comes to mind as I sit down to write this morning is the liberation I feel as a result of Celie's cursing her husband later in the book. I am not saying that all husbands should be cursed, but suddenly I feel—I may wait on men, serve them and enjoy the service, and love them—husbands, sons, friends, but damn it, I am sick and tired of WAITING FOR men. I'm movin' on.

> I tend, as do my sisters, to hold myself on the ready
> to hold open unoccupied territory for a man
> to wait with my work or gifts in hand hoping, hoping, searching,
> waiting expectantly, Will he see and accept?
> or worse: Will he give his okay, so I can go ahead, do my work
> and bring it to him? (Actually, I correct myself here—If I
> truly do my work, I'll have to protect it from him, or perhaps
> too, protect him from it). Not sure what that means.
> If I truly get on with examining what I have to in order to write
> what I must, I will weep and wail and gnash my teeth so much
> that the old happy face will be changed, but, what the hell, it's
> changing anyway whether I give myself to the task or not.

The urge to work like a house of fire rarely comes over me any more.

What's all this waiting for, anyway? Men certainly don't sit around waiting for women, do they? If they do it too, what does the waiting signify? Perhaps a conditioned response of passivity. Waiting to be rescued from having to take up our lives—as Arthur Miller said in *After the Fall*—like an idiot child in our arms.

> This morning I am burning
> with anger, with impatience
> for myself and for all my sisters who wait
> to start living—
> to start being as aggressive about our own lives
> as all of us have been trained that men should be;
> for all the men I love who hold back,
> who refuse to stand at their full height and act
> because they might receive the disapproval of their mothers
> and fathers, they might not turn out as good as
> they have been led to believe they are;
> because they might hurt those entrusted to their care
> and protection, women and children, dependents;
> because all of us might find ourselves dealing in compromise,
> brokenness, tragic choices, places without known rules and

structures, outside the garden, without our precious innocence, without our clothes of righteousness.

AN OUTWARD AND VISIBLE SIGN | Nicki Royall

September 25, 1984
     My mother hates waste. She hates to see people fritter their lives away, squandering energies on useless pursuits. In particular, she hates to see my sisters and me throw ourselves away. She is so afraid, she will do anything to stop us.
     I understand that fear. Each of us daughters have spent huge amounts of energy on "wrong" people. At sixteen, my older sister, Judy, went steady with a French-Canadian flyer named Johnny. He had coal-black hair, steel-blue eyes, a stocky build and macho manner beyond his nineteen years. One May afternoon, Johnny picked up Judy and her friend, Helga, from high school. At a railroad crossing, another car pulled alongside and the drivers exchanged insults. Within minutes, Johnny and the three guys from the other car were fighting. Johnny was stabbed in the neck with a rusty screwdriver.
     My mother was thirty-eight and four months pregnant with my younger sister. She was horrified as Judy and Helga brought Johnny, bleeding, into the house to clean his wounds. After this episode Judy was forbidden to see him again. She was hysterical. She rebelled. Johnny was the great love of her life. She saw no justice in that decision. Over and over, Judy spent her adolescence "guilty by association."
     "You'll end up in the gutter"—the worst, most frequent prophesy my mother invoked. Judy's friends were "ordinary"—a word which in this instance meant less than average. Average is okay. "Ordinary" is low, common, coming from the gutter where Judy might end up.
     Mama sighed with relief when, at seventeen, Judy met Frank, a handsome cadet at a prestigious Virginia military school. Within weeks they were in love. They couldn't contain their passion, and soon they were lovers. That spring, Judy called Frank in a panic when her period was late. He totaled his car coming home to her from college, but was unhurt. They made a secret trip to a nearby city for a pregnancy test, which to their incredible relief was negative.
     But they continued to make love. Each month the fear grew that their luck wouldn't hold. On New Year's Eve, 1960, shortly after midnight, Frank and Judy walked into my parent's party and announced their elopement. They had forged her birth certificate and driven to Elizabeth City, North Carolina, to get married. She was underage at seventeen, he was twenty-one. The relatives gossiped that she "had" to get

married. Why else run off in the middle of her senior year in high school? They never considered Judy's monthly panic and the need to get out from under it.

September 26

My mother's methods of protecting us from wasting ourselves consisted of many questions and conversations about our "dangerous" relationships. Also, she blew up, predictably, every four months or so. Going-off about ten p.m. and exploding through dawn. No one slept through these eruptions. No one escaped her blasts. She saved up hurts for months to spend them all in one night.

My father thought his job during this turmoil was to maintain peace. But whatever peace existed was unsteady at best. Next to my older sister, my adolescence was calm. I was a good student, a member of the National Honor Society, the student senate, Thespians, the literary magazine, homeroom president, etc. My friends and I compared lists of activities in the annual to see who had accumulated the thickest list of accomplishments. Like me, my friends were achievers.

Compared to Judy, my teenage years were downright dull. I had some friends, though, who drove my mother crazy—people who changed me from a friendly, outgoing eighteen-year-old into a withdrawn, sullen woman of twenty-one. Hostile and desperately lonely, I rarely spoke. My mother's greatest fear for me had come true. To my parents, the transformation must have been like watching a yuppie college student turn into a blanked-out, begging moonie.

According to my mother, my "friends" had driven me there. Years later, I realized, to a large extent, she was right. She had an uncanny knack for knowing who was good for me and who wasn't. I had an uncanny knack for zeroing in on who was bad for me.

I wanted to please my mother. At ten, I walked two miles to summer vacation movies on Tuesdays to save bus money. After the feature I bought inexpensive pickle dishes at the "five-and-dime" for her. She still has some. As I got older, my attempts to please her became more elaborate. I entered beauty contests, changed colleges and dressed like Tricia Nixon, all to please her. Even when we argued, at the back of my arguments was the strong desire to pull from her some reassurance that she was proud of me.

October 1

Nineteen. For the first time in my life, a person suggested that my mother's reactions to me might not always be due to some defect in my character. She had to deal with emotional problems from her own upbringing. Until that point, I believed every word she told me about myself in anger. My mother believed that loyalty to parents meant never discussing them with "outsiders." But I formed a close friendship with a girl named Susan. I confided in her about my mother's blowups. But I grew overly dependent on her. She was the only person aware of me in such a total way and who, I thought, accepted me anyway. With everyone else, I felt like a phony. I was a different person with different people. I tried to figure out who they wanted me to be so I could be "it" for them. An antique pillow cover hung framed in my parents' hall: "A friend is one who knows all about you and loves you just the same."

I dropped out of Mary Washington and returned to Christopher Newport. I couldn't concentrate. I re-read the same paragraph again and again without absorbing it. I began to talk to a favorite professor about my problems. Every Monday afternoon, I went to his office for several hours. He arranged joint counseling for my mother and me with a school psychologist, but I felt intensely uncomfortable. I wanted to continue to talk to my professor. So I did for nearly a year. He consulted the psychologist about what we discussed and got back to me the next week with the message. We went on this way until I changed colleges at the end of the semester. I learned a lot from those sessions. Some of my anger and hostility was replaced with sympathy and compassion. But in terms of feeling a genuine sense of self-worth, I had a long way to go. At the core of my being was a secret. A fear, that if the outer layers of my personality peeled away like an onion, the center would hold nothing, or the dark heart of an evil person.

I only respected people who reinforced my bad opinion of myself. Anyone who regarded me highly I judged as either inexperienced or imperceptive. I had an aversion to anyone too "clean cut" or "wholesome." Such people would have nothing in common with me. I saw myself as doomed to unrequited love. I prayed for a savior. Some man to redeem me with his love and save me from my isolation.

I was sure one day I would end up as a shut-in, cut off from friends and the world.

October 7

"In Dreams Begin Responsibilities," a short story by Delmore Schwartz, a young man dreams he is watching his parents' courtship from a movie theater. He senses their deep disappointment in him. His father feels that "Actualities somehow fall short no matter how fine they are."

At first he is in a position of superiority to his mother and father, watching them from fifty stories high; later, lower, on a tightrope, one hundred and fifty feet above their heads. The boy is learning to be less judgmental of his parents. He realizes when he wakes up that he is responsible for his actions. No matter what his mother and father are like—no matter how they have raised him. They are all people, on the same level.

I read this story at nineteen. It was a turning point for me. I identified with the boy so strongly I wrote a paper for my English professor who said I must have fallen in love with the character. But that story opened my eyes. From then on, whatever happened was up to me.

October 21

During my twenty-first year I had a failed romance, I dropped out of college twice, I tried to move to Boston but felt too lonely and unsure of myself to make a go of it. I lived at home. In order to stop being defensive with people, I had deliberately stopped talking and when I needed my voice, I lost it. Whenever I tried to communicate my troubles, my mind blanked.

I had a dream. My face was made of stone. I had three eyes but no mouth. Then I changed into myself again, and I was in bed with an actor who promised to teach me how to make love.

"Please do," I said. "I want so much to know how."

At twenty-two, I took care of my mother for several months while she recuperated from a serious heart attack. I stopped going out much. She didn't like to be alone, and I developed an acute fear of going out myself.

But in April, 1970, I began a job as a social work technician. One week after I started, I decided I was too weak to get out of the house on my own power. It would take too long to earn the money to begin to support myself. Too weak to leave home on my own, too afraid to go out, I felt a desperate need to escape. I didn't want to die, I wanted to be saved—but I was overwhelmed by a sense of impotence. I felt unable to help myself. I took several Qualudes from my mother's prescription and five Visteril tranquilizers. I washed my hair, set it, and left a note.

The next morning I woke up feeling as if nothing had happened—much the same as I felt any morning. I took five more of my mother's Visteril. I went into the bathroom and started to take the curlers out of my hair. In less than a minute I passed out on the bathroom floor.

My ten-year-old sister, Suzi, ran to get my father.

"Nicki's fainted and she's snoring real loud."

As soon as my mother heard I was snoring she said, "Call the rescue squad."

I was rushed to the emergency room. Judy searched my room and found the note. Then she checked my mother's medication and counted them—notifying the hospital—they pumped my stomach.

Everything went black. I had no bodily sensation. A girl's voice yelled "Daddy, Daddy." Many minutes passed before I made the connection that the voice was mine.

Within several hours, I was conscious for awhile although very sleepy. I spent the next few days mostly sleeping. I had not been close to death—but the doctors did say that if I had taken all the medication at once that I took over the course of twelve hours I would have died. What they didn't know was I didn't want to die; I wanted to grow up, be strong and independent, get out of the house.

I regained consciousness in the emergency room. There were apparently enough drugs left in my system to make me extremely sleepy and to lower my defenses. The first person I saw when I came to was my father standing next to me. "Oh, Dad, I want to find someone to love, but even if I did he wouldn't love me because I wouldn't be worthy of it."

I was in the hospital for one week. My psychiatrist made arrangements for me to stay with my married sister. I went back to my new job as a medical aide worker for the local social service bureau.

That was the beginning of several years of intensive psychotherapy for me. At the time I was angry that I should have to undergo therapy when none of the rest of my family was going.

"You are not crazy," my psychiatrist assured me, "just emotionally labile."

All I felt was unhappy and incapable of making a decent decision.

December 2

When I was twelve, I decided to go to confirmation classes in the Episcopal church. Twelve was a religious age for me. I considered several denominations including Presbyterian and Catholic before deciding on the church in which I was raised.

I had to attend the adult classes at night because there were no young people's classes available at the time. I did not want to wait. I went for about six weeks for several hours each class.

I have two main memories from those lessons. The first is that in the early church, women who did not cover their heads were prostitutes. This was the reason behind modern women wearing hats to services. Since this was probably the only piece of "tantalizing" information Father Buck gave us during the whole course, I can understand its fascination for my young mind.

The second memory I have is more a means of expression than a fact. A quote. When talking about the holy communion, Father Buck described the bread and wine as "an outward and visible sign of an inward and spiritual grace."

I want this journal to be an outward and visible sign of my life so far . . . that I want to communicate. That is what I hope to become for myself and for my mother, father, husband, children, friends, teachers, (significant) people in my life. Everyone, in fact. When I look back over the teenage years and the twenties, at the turmoil, desperation, throwing off of false selves, old selves, old values, old ways of dealing with reality—I see it as an inward, spiritual journey toward a hoped-for state of grace. I am not in a state of grace. But I have been given the grace to live this long, to find a certain serenity I hope continues to expand.

I want this book to be a gift to my mother for her life which she may think at times has been wasted. She hurts inside but anyone can see the pain on her face. She has had the grace and the will to withstand it despite the sickness of the spirit that may have brought it on.

I don't think I know the meaning of suffering. Whatever suffering I've done has been largely created by me. I didn't learn how to deal with the world on a more realistic level. I didn't know how to cope. But I've never known hunger. I've always had a place to live. And, despite the lofty expectations I often attach to the word, many people have loved and cared about me. I love them all.

FINDING THE RIGHT FACE   Rebecca McClanahan

April 4, 1984

I'm remembering wanting to be a missionary when I was small. I saw myself living in a grass hut, wearing shapeless cotton dresses, my hair tied back in a clean tight bun. The natives would line up at my tent in the morning, and from my tall canisters I would begin to serve them—saltines, dried fish, Hostess Twinkies for the children. One orange crate would be marked "clothing" and I would pull out dress after dress, ruffles and lace. The little boys would reach for them and begin pulling them over their heads. Everyone wanted to wear the dresses; no one was interested in the corduroy trousers. In my imaginings, they always sit at my feet, their eyes glistening up to me, begging me for Bible stories. A calm comes over me as if I really know what to say to make them happy . . . but they are already happy! That part I never did understand.

June 16

And I really did act out my missionary longings, in my own way. I was always bringing home strays. The puppies who followed me home had scabs. And when I was only three or four, I got my first case of lice. Mom was horrified! Even then, it seemed, I had trouble choosing friends with upward mobility traits. I rolled on the same blanket with a little girl who lived in an apartment, and brought home the lice to prove it. Later, in junior high, I found myself drawn to the outcasts, like Bec Pederson, the hulking eighth-grader who already had a beard. He was in my speech class, and he couldn't get through five words without stuttering. His dark eyes flashed uncontrollably and his whole face twitched. Later I learned that as a small child he had witnessed the murder of his mother by his father, and he had never gotten over it. But even before I knew this, I felt a real sympathy for him. And more than that—I liked him, and it must have shown. The other kids would tease me, running up and down the halls chanting, "Bec and Becky, Bec and Becky!" He did love to sing, though, and later in high school he was accepted into "Debs and Esquires," the most prestigious singing group in our school. I guess I always wanted to take credit for that. Then there was Maureen, that sad-eyed sophomore who walked with a limp. I volunteered to be her partner in tennis. I really liked her. Sometimes, when no one was looking, she would smile at me. Maybe all these were my ways of working out my early missionary longings, the ones I laid aside so easily, though not without guilt, when I discovered the world of men.

March 21

I believe there is something in all of us that wants memories sealed tightly, cleanly. Before it all falls down. The cleanness I felt freshly baptized, a girl with yet no breasts. But the white robe clung to me, and I knew before everyone, God included, I was beautiful and pure. How many Sunday nights I watched the women, the fat-bellied men, the tiny children, enter the tank, disappear, and emerge soaking, the white garments clinging to them. "And this is my beloved son, in whom I am well pleased." How early we learn to please our fathers. Yet I do remember the feeling, and I cannot believe even now, in this whirlwind of doubt, that it was not real—the closest a child can come to dying and being born again, all in one moment. I remember I didn't want my hair to dry. I wanted it to stay forever wet, dripping down my back. This was the sign I had chosen, and I would wear it.

Then one Saturday six years later, it all changed. I had volunteered to help clean the church, and I got the job of cleaning the glass above the baptistry. I didn't want to do it. Something told me not to. Standing there in the dry tank, I saw that it was not a sea, but only a cement tank. The background did not stretch forever to Galilee, the horizon did not extend to the heavens. It was a wallpapering of seas and grasses, plastered over a plain white wall. On either side, dusty plastic ferns sprouted. I could have lived forever and not had to see that. I waited, listening for the flutter of a dove's wing, or at least the movement of waves. Perfectly dry, I stood parched, remembering the white robe clinging to my thighs, wishing again that wetness, praying back the angels.

August 16

Twice this month, I have looked in my bathroom mirror, and my mother stared back. Strange, from a child who tried, but could never trace her mother's nose on her face, or her black hair down her back.

Once needing to know my face shape and thus the image others saw and how to make the most of my best features, which at fourteen I had not yet found, I took a hotel-size bar of Ivory, squinted one eye, and traced my face onto the bathroom mirror. It was hard. You could not be thrown off by your hair (which should be pulled straight back). Block out eyes and mouth, too. Just the shape we're interested in. Draw it and check the box. Square. Rectangular. Heart-shaped. Oval. My square-faced sisters said, "You're so lucky, yours is oval, the classic shape. You can wear any style." I sent off the coupon with the "oval" box checked and they sent me dozens of ideas on how to wear my classic face, but for fifteen years, no matter what I did, I looked the same. Now each time I try to draw the shape of what I am, something jars my hand and I come out lumpy, chin tilted to the right, ears not quite even.

THE BITTER TASTE OF POKE   Judy Hogan

It's dusk. Today, I've had about ten hours, off and on, to write. And as before, as I'm accustomed for it to, my mind is working well and smoothly. Thoughts and images flowing; pieces usually separate, moving together. Today I walked upstream, too, hunting the poke. Looking for the grey hollow stalks that signal that there are roots about to put forth new shoots. I especially looked along the stream. It has a lot of watercress in it, but even though I. says the French believe the presence of watercress is a sign the stream is not polluted, I hesitate to pick it for her. Afraid she'll eat it out of her love for it, unable to resist it when it's present, and then get sick. I'd risk my own health before I'd risk hers. Hers is so precarious. But I'll take her poke. She loved the dandelion greens I fixed with onions, vinegar, and sugar. She'll love the poke. I'll go back Tuesday morning and check the good places. Poke, the finest delicacy of all the wild vegetables. Maybe I shouldn't have bragged so on it, that it was better than asparagus. She knows it, because there's a lot near her son's house in the country. She said the landlady warned him to get it out before the roots clogged up the septic tank. She remembered the purple berries, and thought it pretty obnoxious. It's easy to think of it that way. But once you've eaten "poke salad," your attitude toward the plant changes. How I would love right now to live in the country, for no other reason than to have a fertile brush pile where poke was plentiful in the spring, and blackberry bushes in mid-summer.

I guess in some ways I have made this area my home. So many moves all my life. Yet maybe it is the roots of southerness, after all, that have the strongest tug.

Maybe I do live in the South because of the poke. Not just the poke, but it's a kind of symbol. Cresses are another. I don't really fit in any one culture, or any one place. I'm loose now, in a way, of all social conventions. Inside, which is where it matters. If I want to go gather poke, here, at nine o'clock Saturday morning, no one will stop me. And no one else is gathering it in the meadow at the end of Barclay in Chapel Hill.

How many people can say, "I have lived the way I wanted to?" Not many, I suspect. It is scary. It is still scary to me sometimes. Yet I wouldn't trade it. Everything I've found and learned has been mine. Someone—Frank Lloyd Wright?—said, "What a man does, that he has." My life feels like I have it. I've done it myself, including all the errors and foolishness. All the blind spots and cussednesses. But something in me had that persistent toughness of the poke. That strong thrust up, come spring; come another chance. I suppose, there's a turn in me, too. Fully developed, those purple berries are a potent dye or medicine. Or poison. But the young shoots, "boiled twice to draw the poison out," are a rare delicacy. An "above and beyond," in the natural world. Maybe it pleases me to be able to enjoy and relish a plant known for its poison. The Mother of Transformation knows how to change poison to nourishment.

Eros can also make you sick, or mad. It made my grandmother mad, though I've never been able to get all the details. But her sexual nature would break out, and then, as far as I can guess, she'd feel so guilty and so conflicted, she'd go crazy.

The poison.

But gather and eat the young shoots. Like any fire, love has its uses, and its limits. You will not easily root it out of your heart. But you can learn to harvest it, and draw the poison out, and feast. The phallic nature of the shoots does not escape me either!

I know I prefer East to West because of the feminine landscape, the lushness and density of the vegetation; the insect life at night, especially in the South; and the feeling of an old land warmed easily by sun. Sun is potent here. In Wales, the landscape is even more feminine, because the sun is gentler, and more feminine, and I love Wales more in some ways. But I would miss the poke.

THE PRECIOUS GIFT OF TIME   Elaine Goolsby

January 30, 1981

Snow today. The morning started peacefully enough, with my usual schedule. A few flurries were predicted. Then while I was at work, it really started in. I drove home around noon alone in a world of frozen beauty. I'm fighting despair, depression. Pervading all is a sense the world is mad. We talked of the strong possibility of nuclear war at work today (Brenda, Ray and I) and again at home with Chris tonight. We are, quite literally, sitting on a time bomb. The fruit of the forbidden tree may destroy us yet.

February 6

Today was a good day. Work was productive. But there's a threat of snow and ice again. I'm not ready to drive in that yet! I'm reading Kung and Nouwen, trying to sort out what I believe about Christianity. More and more I sense you don't find it by thinking and looking, but by stillness, by losing the self to find it. I'm alone at home tonight. No radio, no television. Dutchess is curled up beside me on the bed. A precious gift of time. Will I read, write, sort Graham's letters, prepare something for the Sun, revise the Viewing Room poem, sew up the afghan? They all sound splendid. I'll think about it—oh—and drink some tea!

February 8

Early Sunday a.m. One of my favorite times. It's quiet except for a cat fight which I had to extinguish and which really irritated me, encroaching on "my time." I like to sit in my chair, drink coffee and work methodically through the Sunday paper. There are too few quiet moments in my life—so they have great value. Yesterday was a good day with B. D. We had a comfortable, companionable (the nature of our relationship) day with Chinny, who was ecstatic at being included. She sat between us in the truck and took great interest in our destination. We have too few moments like that but the nature of the relationship is intact.

February 13

Lost a dream last night, think it was troubled. Remember wanting to remember it, and I couldn't hold onto it. I'm very tired and stressed and retreat inside my home, my cocoon. Storms swirl, the winter chill seeps in, but the days grow longer and brighter. "Hope is the thing with feathers that nestles in the breast." Emily Dickinson.

March 3

I'm restless, threatened with asthma, have had too much to integrate, I think. Didn't try the CPR training today, knew I couldn't make it physically. Airway—Breath—Circulation, that's powerful stuff, the stuff of life itself. And the Peace College professor died, tied around a tree. What were her last thoughts? Where is she now, on another star? Our clients yesterday, dirty, retarded, on drugs? Four children under six. Pain from so many sources crushing in on me. William Johnson's Christian Zen, the anxiety about looking at ourselves, the terror of the deep.

March 27

Insights gained from reviewing this journal: I'm really caught up in a period of many transitions—major life changes—physically, family, work. Change is inevitable but uncertainty in so many areas is added to that. I'm reeling from it all. This journal process gives me strength, perspective, a place to spill it out. Even the themes of my dreams correlate with the uncertainty. But somehow, with all this, is a faith, an optimism or a certainty that whatever happens will open up new possibilities. Another dream theme is the excitement of being in touch with the creative part of myself. There's so much there. It can be expressed in many ways, in writing, relationships. Whatever happens, that is there. Another theme, being so much more aware of what is happening. This is a mixed blessing for defenses are down a bit, hence the sense of being overwhelmed. Maybe the critical thing is, it all seems to balance out.

October 18

A classic autumn day, gusty, bright colors, quick clouds, then blue sky, leaf and pine needle rain. The needles sting as they make contact. It is dry, the land parched and dry. I've been dry too, in terms of output. Again limited energy coupled with too much to do, and that's pretty much it. I can work, do what I have to at home, and that's it. I've gone through a stack of good escapist books. It's a quiet period. I'm conscious of some things stirring inside—taking on or feeling pain is the crucifixion, the true act of love. This is the pain artists capture in Jesus' eyes. One needs only to look around with open eyes and permit oneself to feel the pain. And we all defend against this very well by pulling the boundaries of our ego tightly around us like the wall of a protective cocoon. The pain is raw in every house on this, and any, street. It's necessary to block some of it out in order to make it. In addition to withdrawing by reading, I'm on an eating binge—cramming with both hands. Must get control of that. And asthma, that too familiar companion is back, mild and controllable, but back and that's discouraging. Am I depressed? Not consciously, but that's certainly what I'm describing, the clinician notes. To sin and switch metaphors, sometimes the pain breaks through defenses like waves through a sea wall. This journal is laced with the theme of not enough time/energy to do more than exist. Yet I know I do a lot—I'm a competent mother, wife, professional, companion/sitter to my handicapped mother, sometimes writer. I will have to do the best I can with what I have, time and energy, and not obsess about what I can't do.

GOOD DOGGIE, BAD DOGGIE | Beth Ellen McLain

January 14, 1984

Alan and I toured J. P. Stevens' Whitehorse Plant number one today. It was most interesting, though I have been in a cotton mill many times before. Alan had never been in one before; I think he was fascinated by all of the loud machinery and seeing the process from raw cotton to cloth.

The tour brought back memories of my days as a winder operator in a cotton mill in Albemarle. I would not have believed it at the time, but those were some of the best days of my life (also some of the worst). Life was much simpler then. I worked midnight until 8:00 every day, but I didn't have the pressure that college causes; I also didn't have the pride in myself that I sometimes find here. My sister, brother, a friend from high school, and I all worked together at the cotton mill for a summer. We made the best of it and really had a pretty good time. But now we are all separated, hundreds of miles apart. Sometimes it hurts a little; no, a lot. People move out of your life and others come in and (try to) take their place, I guess that's how it is supposed to be. They never tell you that one day you will lose the people you love the most; death doesn't always take them away; sometimes it is simply miles that separate us.

February 7

Jill, Bobby and I went to Fayetteville to pay our last respects to Mr. W. I spent an hour and a half observing the reactions of people at a funeral home. I didn't really know the people there, but it was interesting to watch, as an outsider looking in. It was most touching to see Mrs. W. view her husband's body. She walked to the casket and looked sadly at the body, then she reached down and rubbed his chest. As she walked away, she lovingly patted him goodbye. Kevin, the grandson, also touched me deeply. He spent most of his time leaning on the casket crying. He looked at his grandfather and seemed to be thinking, "You're not really dead, you can't be, I don't want you to be dead." Every now and then, he would lay his head down on the American flag which covered the casket and cry softly into his open hands. It was a sad sight, it almost moved me to shed a tear or two. But I was strong, like always, and held it in until the feeling went away.

For the most part, the other people seemed as if they were at a social gathering, or a party. The only difference was that the shell of a wonderful man, gone to meet his maker, lay in the same room.

March 8

Tammy and I cleaned up her dorm room this afternoon because her old roommate is coming to visit the week after break. We got down on our hands and knees and scrubbed her floor with ammonia. It was really fun. I put on my old overalls and looked just like a regular maid. In class, I look like the average student, (well, maybe not) but when I put my overalls on, I'M SUPER MAID! Tammy and I enjoyed it so much that we discussed quitting school and getting a job scrubbing floors. The pay is good, and the job is so rewarding. I don't know why we're wasting our time and money going to college when we could get a real job scrubbing floors. Here we are spending good money to have some professor tell us to write a term paper or read a book. What I say is, "If he wants the paper written, let him write it himself. He is the one getting paid, not me."

It's just like my brother; he had a good job in a cotton mill, making good money. He was a filling hand, and they were going to promote him to one of them fancy jobs, like doffer, or something. But what does he do, I'll tell you what he does. He quits to go back to one of them institutions of higher mind polluting. He thinks an honest job making honest money ain't good enough for him. He wants to go back to school and let them educated dummies put more crazy ideas in his head. Well, I'll tell you one thing, it's communist. I ain't goed to school pass the six grade, but I done all right for myself. That education don't do nothing but pollute your mind. They go to school and next thing you know, they want to learn to dance. Everybody knows that dancing ain't nothing but convulsions caused by demons being in you. Well, I'm going to stay away from that stuff.

June 21

I screwed up big time today. It all started when I figured out a clever way of getting out of doing my oral presentation in economics class. On Friday, we were to turn in our current event report and do a couple minutes oral presentation about it. A few days ago, I decided that I would finish my report on Wednesday, turn it in on Thursday, and tell the teacher that I wouldn't be able to be in class on Friday. That is exactly what I did, but it didn't work out as planned. Today after economics class I went up and told Mrs. C. that I wanted to turn in my report early because I couldn't be in class on Friday. She was very nice about it. She told me that it was fine and that I could do my oral presentation on Monday because the oral presentation was a requirement.

I don't know how I always manage to get myself into these messes, but I do. I feel like a little doggie who has just chased a car and knows she has to go back to her master and take her punishment. If only I hadn't chased that stupid car I wouldn't be in the mess I'm in now. But I did, so now I have to be a good doggie and take my punishment. Of course, I could do like my little dog, Toby, used to do. When he chased a car, he knew that as soon as he got back home he would be punished. So, instead of coming right home, he would take the long way around Palestine, thinking that by the time he got home we would have forgotten all about it. That's a good idea; should I be a good doggie or a bad doggie?

HUNGER LIKE A PLANT TO BLOOM | Agnes McDonald

February 9, 1985
　　Woke up in relief. I am not married to W. P. I am not married to anybody. It was a dream! I feel as if I have just been commuted from a prison sentence. Succotash or Stocking, I think I'll call her that. It's a cute name. I love her one orange paw. She is overseeing this writing project.

February 11
　　News of more rain and snow. I am a frail vessel that my barometer perches so precariously on the sweeps and swings of weather. My pale skin, my flesh like a sponge wants to soak the sun, and press myself against the smells and feel of spring. How we hunger like plants to bloom, to move inexorably to the next cycle we have grown accustomed to. We are still so primitive in this way, and thank God that planetary pulls and pushes and pulses, tides, waxes and wanes still wrap us in their clothes.
　　I rebel by wasting time, at least I have gotten better about wasting money. Why do I have to waste anything, particularly time? Of such value. I cannot any more truthfully say, I don't have time. Because I do. It's better to say, I don't want to have time. But why? Like yesterday. I wanted time to myself. But why time to do nothing? Just to stare into space. I could have done something. But I wanted nothingness, just to say, now, it's mine and I'll do exactly what I wish with it, so there. Even if it's bad for me.
　　Going shopping on Saturday. The onslaught of wedding, love, romance, sights, smells, satin hearts, lace, Giorgio, string quartets, people, transactions, lush draperies, silk nightgowns. I felt instantly caught up in this flood, and had to get away, to get out of it. It was too tempting, too sensuous, and yet in a way disgusting to me. On the one hand, I felt deprived, like Christ tempted in the wilderness, and I had brought my wilderness with me. I do not know how much of the luxurious in my life is okay. As much as I can "afford," I guess. I'll know when the cost gets too high. And yet so many parts in me and my value system say no, this is child's play, a toy to put away now. I wish I could get rid of this part in myself, this insatiable maw, this animal I have to

keep on a leash, keep always at bay, who strains and salivates and obsesses about certain kinds of luxury, a craving which cannot be satisfied, like ambition. I wish I could amputate that part of myself, wear blinders, inside. Some people do, or seem to. These things just don't matter. Wrestling with these devils is not their chore.

February 12

So what do I want that I'm not getting? Abundance. That's what Nouwen writes about. See it all as plenty to go around. Get over the childish way of seeing relationships as rationed or economical encounters. Thinking there's just a little to go around. And yet I waste, profligate that I am, time, money, my own resources. How hard it is to be "a channel of light, a channel of love." It is impossible. I am clogged. My channels are dim and hazardous, and what passes through is watered down and tepid, and often blocked. I want perfection now. But patience is not one of my virtues. Passivity, yes, patience, no. At least it has been good for me to write it down. The clean white sheet of paper, the *tabula rasa*, we are never this. But only what we write upon it, with grace.

February 19

. . . the urges inappropriate and unacceptable that shook me and obsessed me from time to time, and of the men who were attracted to me. I think I must have thought this was my fault. A childish way to see this, and typically my tendency to blame myself as the center of the universe. Of course it was not my fault, some fatal or dark taint, some seductive spell I cast without knowing or meaning to. That's just what some men have liked to blame on women down through history. "There I was minding my own business, when this Eve creature sidled up to me and I just couldn't help myself." I really believe I bought it, too. It fit right in with the way I have blamed myself for other things.

I realize that other people, men, have their own processes, their own drives, their own realities; they move toward me, I move toward them. We are like atoms, highly charged in an energy field which is time and place, all we are and have been. We can resist, we can give in, move toward, move away. Notably, it is not one person, I, in charge or in control, men being helpless prey falling. They are people like me, driving and being driven. They are as much responsible as I. It's like they are part of this universe of planetary bodies, all of us orbiting, powered by who we are, both what we know about who we are and what we don't know.

Some of us are driven more by one, some more by the other. But although I was "taught" that my sexuality had great effect or power, could do all sorts of things to people, almost as if by magic, I never felt this power. It always seemed to be going outward, to people out there. Not staying even a little bit in me, so that I've had a hard time feeling sexual unless someone out there agreed I was. So really no one had any real power, in a way.

Men, seeming like Mother said, like little boys, you had to act right, or you tried not to do anything to turn them on or excite them. Of course, this is exactly what is the popular reason why women get raped. You shouldn't have worn that tight sweater. It all fits in.

This doesn't mean you have no responsibility, but only for yourself, not for everyone else in the world. This is sort of my repudiation of the flypaper theory of sexual guilt, and it works so well, because the flypaper has no control over its stickiness. And flies can be forever condoned for their fatal encounter. What could they do? This way no one really has any power, and no one has a fighting chance. And it's all done with words, and it's all done to us so young.

We all carry so much baggage around this part of our lives, and the chances of running into someone quirky or dangerous, or just loaded down with a lot of stuff not related to his/her partner at all, seems very likely.

It's a strange world. You can't go around looking over your shoulder all the time or you'll never see where you are going. And yet if you don't watch out somewhat, you could get broken into a million pieces.

I am really hurting now. I have pulled off enough scabs in this writing to amount to a real wound.

I feel like everything I touch in my professional, artistic life turns to gold, and everything in my romantic life, turns to shit. In fact, I suspect romance is shit.

February 27

Today Maggie and I drove to Cedar Island, playing Willie Nelson on the tape player at top volume. What beauty. Incomparable. "Nature is only a cry of God." Well, ain't that something? The daffodils are blooming boldly, not holding anything back, with pizzazz, as Annie Dillard says, and violets blooming in a yard of grassy hummocks. When you are gotten by God, you are gotten good. The mallards and drakes waiting by the banks, watching and waiting for the baby ones to swim. Knowing they will. It's their being, their nature. The immense expanse of wheat-colored grasses stretching into infinity, the sound of their rustling. Maggie says, "Listen! The sound of the grasses?" The voices of the grass choir, singing a song like no other, in tune, in harmony, the music of silent tears. And where the road ends. There are ends to roads, but always a way back, not the same, yet the same. But you can't help but go back. The layers of non-feeling and public life sloughing off. Why do we work so hard to become blind and deaf, to crowd out the ecstatic splendor of creation, to cover it up, to cement it over, signs and symbols of man everywhere, but love, it surges through somehow, with a little "help," like the ducks who "help" their young ones to become what they are, simply by being there. And so we go back to the familiar world, taking what we have learned, back to others. To testify to the glory and the majesty and the power. Like Kasas' horses. He paints the very fire that destroyed his house, canvas after canvas, he painted out of his pain, out of his very flesh, and then his horses, their redeeming power, the Lawrentian sexual drive to make it through the storm. Horses in the field. In rain.

And this same day I find my "A" in a junky garbage dump of a fish factory and packing house, boat yard. My initial written in weathered wood on the ground, big. It would have been hard to miss. I look down. There it is. The Alpha, the Beginning. In the beginning was the Word. I have always loved these words, although I do not understand them. Maybe because I do not understand them. I want to cry. I want to cry. Like coming home, like food when we are hungry, love when we are so far from love we don't even know we want it. That is when it gets frightening. How long can we fly on automatic pilot? That flight is not the flight we need. It's when we yield to our hearts, that the flight takes us where we need to go.

ALPHA COMPANY	Jean Niedert

October 10, 1987

I realized my problem is I am experiencing a vast amount of disillusionment in all aspects of my life. Work—or my existence at work— is meaningless. We are viewed as cogs in the machine. With all these personal games going on in upper management, we're all pawns.

At times, I feel invisible. Life goes on without me. People are there, yet I'm not recognized and it bothers me. I'm meaningless.

October 17

I enjoyed my day off. The most eventful thing was visiting the moving wall, a half-size replica of the Vietnam Veteran's Memorial. As I walked down the path, it was interesting to see the people coming from the opposite way. Wondering why they came, what they were feeling. Did they know someone on the wall? Did they know more than one? I walked the wall, pausing at the panels, observing the people. One lady was doing a pencil rubbing of a name and said, to nobody in particular, "He has a little baby he's never seen." One man sat in the grass about fifteen or twenty feet from a particular panel. There were single roses. There was a handful of yellow wild flowers. There was a letter on the ground perched up against the wall. I walked further and listened to the veterans talk about their experiences with other veterans, telling each other when they were over there. One said something about being there until '68, how he came home and fought the war until '75 and is still fighting it. My eyes watered—thinking of all these people—thinking about the book *Chickenhawk* and knowing that all those people in the book—all of them who died—were somewhere on the wall. And out of all those names, I knew not one. And I'm thankful that I didn't know anyone on that wall. People touched names, and stared at them for eternity. I never touched the wall. It felt too personal to touch.

I walked by the letter I had seen earlier. The wind had blown it facing up. I looked hard to see what was written on it. It was addressed to "Alpha Company." I couldn't believe it. You have to wonder what that letter said.

I didn't want to walk away.

January 13, 1988

Driving home tonight, I realized this has been the longest week of my life. I look forward to the weekend when I don't have to spend half the day in traffic and all day dreading driving. It's unrelenting—there is no telling when the snow will melt and the roads will be dry and clear.

I stopped by the library and picked up the only books they had available on the Vietnam War. While looking at those pictures, I realized those soldiers could be guys I knew. They were all so young, and here they are covered in mud—having to live in it. I cannot get over how they were treated. I am only just beginning to learn about the war, and I am amazed how little I knew. Before 1986, or for sure 1987, I had probably awareness of only one per cent of the war. That's not right. We should have learned about it in school. It's pretty obvious why those veterans have the feelings of betrayal. I would feel the same if I lived in the mud, saw death and hate.

Just driving in the snow has been a living hell for me—it's the most stress and fear I've experienced for a long period of time. And It's a blink of an eye compared to their experiences. Their "hell" never ended. At least I could find relief at home. They had no home. And what's so very sad is they deserve so much—but it's too late—there's nothing I can do to make it up to them. And that's the saddest thing of all.

April 14

I found Alpha Company! I think I found the man who wrote the letter!

Alpha Company was mentioned in the "PM Magazine" segment, "Letters from Nam." I knew it was coming. The clues went as follows: Phil Woodall was there twenty years ago. He left in '67, returned in the spring of '68. They talked about the company and Lieutenant Gary

Scott. My mind asked, "Could this be Alpha Company?" They showed the letter Phil wrote—it could be the writing on the envelope I saw at Freedom Park. They showed the company—a picture. All the time I knew and kept waiting, hoping they'd tell the company, and they did. I screamed.

Alpha Company has been found! The reason for the letter might be near. I know a little about Alpha Company. There was an ambush.

April 15

I bought *Letters Home From Vietnam* today. I think I puzzle people about why Alpha Company is so important to me. Since October, Alpha Company has been in my thoughts. Wondering what happened to them. Wondering why a letter was written to an entire company. The more research I do, the more tragic it seems.

All I know is there is something out there. Somehow there is a reason why I've been made aware of the Vietnam War and Alpha Company. The chance observation of the letter, the chance of missing homecoming and going to Freedom Park to see the wall alone, the need to write what I felt. The twelve inches of snow that kept me snowbound in January, inspiring me to press on. The ghosts that convinced me to press on to learn about myself. The need to do something about myself. The need to do something at the twenty-year observation and the disappointment of not doing it. And then, again by chance, watching "PM Magazine" only to find more answers, gaining more fuel to push me onward.

If anything, recent events only reinforce the fact that there are stories to write. There are stories I am supposed to write. At this point, I do not know exactly what the subject matter is but I do know my mission is to write. I know it as clearly as I know my name. And what is so exciting is that writing satisfies me. It gives me an outlet to my honesty. It frees my soul of all it feels. Whereas socializing is such a farce, when I write it is me, my soul, my feelings that hit the page and sound out my personality. And I can write without fear of rejection because if I feel it's right, it is right for me. The adventure is discovering the subject matter and putting it in words. Words and thoughts that are unique to me.

April 20

For the past two days, I've found it hard to go to sleep. I've also been totally engrossed in *Dear America, Letters Home from Vietnam*. My heart goes out to so many of them. But one guy's letters—Marion Lee ("Sandy") Kempner—stuck out. One regarding the observation of a flower without thorns and relating it to life. Stood out like a star in the night. I *really* liked it. Plus, as he talked about this flower existing on a hill, it was a full circle about his existence. He died on November 1, 1966. He talked about people not seeing the flower, except for him and his buddy, yet the flower will "achieve a sort of immortality" because it will always live in the memory of the "tired, wet Marine." And now the flower continues to live, as does the soul of Sandy. It's almost comforting. Just like the envelope addressed to Alpha Company, this letter touches my heart, it communicates emotions, thoughts that are deep.

I came across another letter that I enjoyed—this one made me smile. I turned to see who wrote it, only to find it was from Sandy. He was so witty, so full of life in his letters, yet so thoughtful, too.

Now that I've become focused again, life is good. I know that there are stories to write. I can see them develop in my mind. Currently, they're ideas and single thoughts. I will be building from observations. And lately, especially this past week, I've really noticed how I am observant of small details: blossoms on a tree, birds, the spring green of the oak trees, the new growth on the holly trees. It's small things that bring a surprise of wonderment to the day.

July 13

As I drove into my apartment complex, I stopped at the mailbox. Something said maybe the letter would be there, plus I wanted *Adweek*. It was there, a letter from Phil Woodall. I brought it home—anxious to read the words, yet scared. I have been thinking about what my letter might have brought to PW. It's amazing what a letter can do.

As I read and reread the letter, I got out my Vietnam folder and organized the information. Looked it over. In my mind, I know there is one *powerful* story that is developing.

It's scary. But again, it's exciting. There is potential for a new beginning, a threshold of discovery. Of course, there's the possibility of losing my innocent views. I have read books on Vietnam and have based opinions, developed theories and meaning from my point of view. Quite different from one who has seen war, seen the evil and sorrow that war inflicts on people. And here I am, one who sees things differently at different angles. But I do know that there is a reason for me to be here, at this point. The events which occurred wouldn't have happened like they did had there not been a reason.

As I looked through my Vietnam folder, I found a scrawl of frustration that stated, "The possibility of finding Alpha Company is rare." Well, not only did I find the right one, I found the writer of the words, also. Amazing.

I am scared. There is a lot of awful stuff that went on in Vietnam. Am I ready for it? I don't think you can be (just as the soldiers couldn't have been). So much swirls in my thoughts . . . but sleep is calling.

OVER THAT FAR HILL   Mary Kratt

December 4, 1984

Because of the airline's cheap ticket requirements, I'm here early, so I have breakfast with a friend of an acquaintance. I called her on the phone and we meet at something like a Holiday Inn. Never in the South have I seen a harp player at a motel buffet on a Sunday morning. We talk of the woman we know in common and stories about the campus, how Carl Sagan lives in a rock house on one deep stone gorge nearby above the cascading water, how the Cornell and White (founding patriarchs) statues met one night in the center of the quad they've surveyed for one hundred years, shook hands and went back to watch another hundred. That explained the footprints I saw painted near the base of Cornell's statue. How she laughed to learn they were still there from her youth. And I almost stayed here without knowing about them. Self-guided tourists often miss the lore which makes places rich and human.

I listened about her job and troubles, her husband with multiple sclerosis, nothing self-pitying. She has come to terms with it and tells of her four children and how two live with them while waiting to find jobs. I am always amazed how women plunge into the personal with such unselfconscious immediacy. Old friends do it, of course. This woman will never see me again. Women are often so honest, it's enough to make you lay down your life for them on the spot. Giving themselves away is what so many of them are used to.

She lets me out, and I go back to my life and she returns to hers. She hopes to change jobs soon. I walk to the places she pointed out from the car. I'm wearing far too many clothes. The far north is not as cold as I thought. It is sleeting slightly, streets icy earlier, now turn to mush. Everyone goes as if it is nothing. It is. Another grey, slushy day in Ithaca. Williams Street is as steep as any I've ever seen.

I am happy. I hike in my boots to the I. M. Pei-designed museum and spend several hours there. The tall white pillar of glass windows is out of place, many would say, among this antique architectural potpourri, but once you are inside, it earns its difference. On each floor and from the top, where the view is splendid. A pole sculpture, like an askew teepee, marks the yard below among other modern artworks. Still further below is the town and Cayuga Lake and mists lifting and falling rapidly to show the far hills beyond.

I get fussed at in front of a Georgia O'Keefe for using a ballpoint pen to write on my museum guide. So I memorize the names there, the pictures in that corner: Mary Cassett, Elaine de Kooning and nearby Margaret Bourke-White, Berenice Abbott, Steichen, Louise Nevelson, Imogen Cunningham, amazing pictures and work. And I find Christmas cards—western photos by Ansel Adams and a few of Whitman sitting by an open window like a New England sage on a Tuesday morning. This is Whitman country — Elmira nearby.

I am wearing a great old Navy-issue pea coat and it is hot, the sweat of climbing wets my back, but I'm afraid to leave it anywhere, so I endure it. The most amusing exhibit is the main one, Michael Snow, who obviously got stuck in his life for about seven years by one woman's shape and silhouette crossing a street. It is shown in all possible media and materials throughout one floor, and one view even resembled what might possibly be her innards. You have to say he certainly persisted and carried out a creative theme to original fruition, but was it worth it? When he got to the quadruples of her in large aluminum women, I went to find the Asian collection.

I could not get enough of the scene out of every vista of those high windows. The angles and light at every turn make me yearn for my own camera. But when I carry it, I see differently and am preoccupied by it and its own eye, so on certain voyages I leave it behind to use my interior camera. To try to see for writing and to photograph simultaneously is like wearing your eyes on your ears or a shoe on your nose. Down below me, through the window, I see a photographer's picture, footprints criss-crossing snow between winter trees within the frame of walkways, one student's red scarf hangs whimsically over a pole of the sculpture, the only dot of color in the entire landscape.

Then I found the suspension bridge over the Cascadilla falls, resembling closely some of the steep river walls and the town of Baden in West Germany, all dark and wintry, their rock trails closed and treacherous now. They tell me the old movie, *Perils of Pauline* was filmed here. And that graduate students take this leap in desperation sometimes. There is a dire finality about it. A compelling invitation. The bridge sways in the wind and I watch the water raving, falling far below two hundred feet, sheer rock sides and trees and this open mesh metal bridge, which makes security imaginary. And the campus wedged between this gorge on the west and one by my room on the east. Two great fissures and tumbling water. The more I travel, the more I see history begins with geography. I thought of Cornell all my life as an institution. It is indigenous to this rock and water. Its very character. So much always goes back to the land.

Standing here alone over the chasm, I wonder what this forty-seven-year-old woman — married, mother of three, six hundred miles from home, standing on a sleeting Sunday over a wintry cataract in a northern town, closer to Canada than Carolina, what am I doing here alone? Using the library manuscript collection tomorrow, yes. Seeing the world, yes. New, wonderful places like a late-life explorer. There are only young students everywhere with their parkas and boots and backpacks. An occasional male professor with his children on a weekend afternoon. No one like me. Perhaps they are home watching a movie or game or doing laundry, while I taste the world's variety. A raccoon peeks his long nose up from underneath a street drain's grating on the roadway near the gorge.

I call home on a pay phone and tell of my wonderful day, how it is dark at 4:30 and I have eaten supper already and will continue with my *New York Times* and set my clock to be climbing the library hill by 7:45 a.m. I'll wake in the dark, eat my orange and half bagel and be there. Yes! Lucky to have lived long enough and found enough loving freedom to do this. How many centuries have women wanted to go over that far hill? I thank God in heaven and my own father and mother and husband and my own self for risking it, for imagining it was possible.

WHERE I AM HEADED   Kendall

December 22, 1984

I sit back on my big couch munching fruitcake, sipping coffee and stretching, while the sun rises. I lick a crumb of candied pineapple off my thumb, suck morsels of pecan out of my teeth and review the last two days.

Thursday took Seth to the airport in a cab. He goes to Arizona, to his grandparents, at their expense. I will join him there in a few days. It was a foggy damp morning, and he and I were tired of our struggles and glad to separate. Left the airport on foot in blue sweatshirt, jeans, sneakers; walked to a bus stop on Martin Luther King Boulevard, across the street from a barbecued ribs place loud with black men celebrating the holidays cheerfully already. Thought how much I hate the whiteness of this city: how far away the black folks live from the whites, how far away the black world is from these rich students with their cars and condos. How I ache for greens & cornbread & black laughter & gospel. How fucking pale the white world is, cradled in wealth and protected from life by dollar bills. I think when I leave here I will go to Washington, D. C., and teach in an urban college. Or Chicago. If they will have me. Somewhere there are poor people who still fight for the chance to get an education, as I have fought, as I still do. Somewhere there are old women, like me, struggling to know something with life under their belts and children hanging off their arms. I will leave the white Texas world behind me, glad of what I got from it, glad of what I gave, but knowing Texas is not the South. And the South is angry, smoldering. And I am probably not going to quit falling in love. And I had better get my act together, if I'm going to be of any use to anyone before I die. I will find my people. I wonder if C. will go with me. I wonder if anything this good can last. I'm so dumb, so blank. I know less than I have ever known, but I will be of use.

March 29, 1985
I have this fantasy, that I meet my great-grandmother, Sophia, dead long before I was born. I meet her and know her, take her hand as another strong woman, and we go forward together. I see her, an intelligent woman denied education by a world in which women were not supposed to think; I see Sophia, and my Russian Jewish great-grandmother in the wheat fields, the women in log cabins with tired eyes, the women who dreamed and imagined what it would be like to read, to write. Me and my crowd. They put me at the front of the V, they form a wedge behind me. We move together, black, brown, Jewish, white, big-bellied with babies, cooking and sewing, loving other women and loving men. My training is almost over. I am about to begin forward motion that only I can see. What they have prepared me for. There are questions to be asked to this man's world, where bombs are worth more than education or welfare or the health of black babies. We will be asking them. I will be helping my people ask these questions. I didn't come all this way to assimilate with the white boys. From those suburban houses where I grew up, houses seething with sadism, twisted heterosexual sex, hatred: seething with materialism, anger, violence. To this sense of commitment to my people, to our education out of the drugged stupidity of our days. We have some questions to ask of the white boys.
I put on my great-grandmother's posture. In my mind, I take on her force, her certainty of being right, her protectiveness, her power. My grandmother's black dress. And, by God, I *march*. And she, and the others, and their kids, boys too, we form a column. We're going to rock the boat, and set lots of boats rocking. We're going to churn up the sea, as much as we can. Look out, status quo. This is a radical column coming through. If I can only remember where I mean to be going. If I can just not forget, in the going there, where I am headed.

CONTRIBUTORS

Joy Averett grew up on a tobacco farm near Oxford, North Carolina. A secondary school teacher for more than 30 years, she died in April 1991.

Jane Beed is the pen name of Betsy Sayre, who has made the life and work of Pearl S. Buck her study. A graduate of Randolph-Macon Women's College in Lynchburg, Virginia, she volunteers with the American Association of Retired Persons VITA tax assistance program for elderly and low income individuals.

Rita Berman was born and educated in England. She has published a reference book, *The A-Z of Writing and Selling*, as well as more than four hundred feature articles, interviews and travel columns.

Betsy Blair was born in Charleston, South Carolina and grew up in Augusta, Georgia. She has a B.A. in English from Agnes Scott College, and an M.A. in Product Design from North Carolina State University.

Susan Broili, a native of Durham, North Carolina, has worked as a journalist at the *Herald-Sun Newspapers* for fifteen years. She has published fiction, poetry and art criticism. She has been the recipient of an Emerging Artist Grant from the North Carolina Arts Council and, in the fall of 1992, she traveled to Russia as part of a writers' exchange.

Lynn Bunis received a B.A. from George Mason University and an M.S. in Sociology from the American University. She is an editor who lives with her husband in Bethesda, Maryland and she enjoys quilting.

Pauline Cheek, a native of Durham, North Carolina, received a B.A. from Wake Forest University, a M.A.T. from Duke University, and an M.Div. from the Earlham School of Religion. She has published articles in Appalachian *Heritage, Now And Then, Mountain Living,* and *Southern Exposure.*

Shirley Cochrane is a poet and fiction writer who lives and teaches in Washington, D.C. She is the author of a fictionalized memoir entitled *Everything That's All* (Signal Books).

Stella C. Cook is a native of Suffolk, Virginia, who enjoys wildlife, the woods, gardening and the freedom she experiences through her journal writing.

Judy Goldman lives in Charlotte, North Carolina and works as a public radio commentator and poetry instructor. She is the author of a collection of poetry, *Holding Back Winter* (St. Andrews Press) and *Wanting to Know the End* (Silver Fish Review Press), winner of the 1992 Gerald Cable Poetry Chapbook Prize.

Elaine Goolsby grew up on a tobacco farm in the northern Piedmont of North Carolina and now lives in Durham, North Carolina. She is the co-author of *Letter in a Bottle* (Carolina Wren Press).

Jaki Shelton Green is the author of *Dead on Arrival and New Poems*, and *Masks* (both by Carolina Wren Press). A Community Economic Development Specialist in Hillsborough, North Carolina, she has performed her poetry, conducted workshops, and served as writer-in-residence in the United States and Europe. Her poems have appeared in *Essence, Ms.,* and *African-American Review.*

Robin Greene, a native of New York state, has an M.A. in English and an M.F.A. in Writing. She teaches English and Literature at Methodist College in Fayetteville, North Carolina, and is the author of *Memories of Light* (1991).

Gwynne Hackworth, a native of Florida, is an active member of the National Association of Women.

Jane Hanudel lives with her husband and two sons, and works part-time in her husband's law office. She enjoys writing poetry and sewing.

Betty Hodges, who lives in Durham, North Carolina, has worked on a journal for half a century and is at work on an autobiographical novel, an outgrowth of encountering Proust's treatment of hidden memory. She has written a literary review column continually since 1955 for the *Herald-Sun Newspapers.*

Judy Hogan, a writer and poet living in Saxapahaw, North Carolina, is the author of several books, including *Light Food* (1989) and *Watering the Roots in a Democracy* (Carolina Wren Press).

Janis Holm, Associate Professor of English at Ohio University, is the author of several publications, including a critical edition of Bruto's *The Mirrhor of Modestie* and exploratory essays on early modern English prescriptive literature for women.

Lu Ellen Huntley-Johnston grew up in Wadesboro, North Carolina. She received an M.A. from Middlebury College and is a doctoral candidate at N.C. State University. She is currently on the faculty of the Department of English at the University of North Carolina at Wilmington.

Lorraine Hutchins is a native of Washington, D.C. She is a freelance writer and editor.

Sue Lile Inman, a native of Little Rock, Arkansas, currently lives in Greenville, South Carolina, where she is a freelance writer.

Kendall has lived in the South for more than thirty years. An avocational writer, actress, drama teacher and journal writer, she also enjoys writing plays and book reviews.

Mary Kratt is a North Carolina writer whose books of lively stories, poetry and biography are filled with humor and regional history. She received a B.A. from Agnes Scott College and is the author of *The Only Thing I Fear is a Cow and a Drunken Man* (Carolina Wren Press).

Glorianna Locklear grew up on a one-mule farm in South Carolina. She recently received a doctorate and is on the faculty of Winston-Salem State University.

Nancy Markham was born in Durham, North Carolina, and now lives in Sunnyvale, California. She is on the faculty of the Humanities of San Jose State University.

Rebecca McClanahan lives in Charlotte. She is author of *Mrs. Houdini* and *Mother Tongue* (University Presses of Florida), and *One Word Deep: Lectures and Readings*. She is a recipient of a North Carolina Fellowship and the PEN Syndicated Fiction Award.

Agnes McDonald, a native of Durham, North Carolina, is the author of a poetry collection, *Quickest Door, Smallest Room* (St. Andrews Press, 1992). She has published poetry and reviews in numerous publications including *Southern Poetry Review* and *Carolina Quarterly*.

Beth Ellen McLain lives in Albemarle, North Carolina, where she works as a reporter and columnist for the *Stanly County News and Press*. A graduate of Pfeiffer College, she has published poetry in *Carolina Voices* and *Phoenix*.

Brenda Murphree was born in Jackson, Mississippi and lived as a child in both South Carolina and Tennessee. She describes herself as a "regular old kind, you know, serious writer. Literary stuff. I am not a journalist."

Jean Niedert grew up on Florida's Space Coast watching launches thunder into the sky. She currently lives in Charlotte, North Carolina, where she is a freelance copywriter.

Kristin Petersen lives with her seven-year-old daughter in Raleigh, North Carolina, where she works as a graphic designer and writer for non-profit organizations.

Jo Jane Pitt believes that life is a spiritual quest and that her work is to leave the planet a little better for having been here.

Vicki Posey, born and raised in Georgia, is an adjunct instructor teaching writing and literature at Wesleyan and St. Mary's Colleges. Her short story, "The Stain," appeared in a collection, *What's a Nice Girl Like You Doing in a Relationship Like This*.

Jacklyn Potter, a writer and teacher in Washington, D.C., has her poetry and translations in such books and publications as *If I Had My Life to Live Over, I'd Pick More Daisies* (Papier-Mache Press), *Gargoyle, Washington Review, Stone Country, Sou'wester, Poet Lore*, and *The Stones Remember, Native Israeli Poetry* (Word Works Press).

Lynn Powell, from Chattanooga,Tennessee, has taught poetry and fiction writing at Cornell University, and Ithaca College, and conversational English to children in Puerto Rico.

Becke Roughton, a native of North Carolina, teaches creative writing and fine arts at James Sprunt Community College in Kenansville, North Carolina. Currently at work on an M.F.A. in Writing at Warren Wilson College, she is editor of *Wellspring*.

Eleanor Roland is "a middle-aged African-American woman of southern origin who aspires to write." She says she is a feminist *and* a humanitarian.

Nicki Royall, who lives in Williamsburg, Virginia, is author of a non-fiction book entitled, *You Don't Need to Have a Repeat Caesarean* (1983).

Susan Schmidt teaches writing, literature and interdisciplinary environmental courses at the North Carolina School of Science and Mathematics in Durham, North Carolina. She is the recipient of a 1993-94 National Endowment for the Humanities Fellowship to study environmental literature. Her work has included stints as an environmental policy analyst, science journalist and sailboat captain.

Nancy Simpson lives in the mountains of western North Carolina. Her chapbook, *Across Water*, and a full-length poetry collection, *Night Student*, were published by State Street Press.

Alice Sink, who lives in Lexington, North Carolina, is an Associate Professor of English at High Point University. She is a book reviewer for the *Greensboro News and Record* and a member of the Board of Directors of the North Carolina Writers' Network. Her essay, "Sundays," was published in *Bottomfish* (1992).

Anita Skeen, currently on the faculty of Michigan State University, is a native West Virginian who completed her undergraduate work at Concord College. She is the author of two collections of poetry, *Each Hand a Map* and *Portraits*. She has recently completed a book of short stories and is currently at work on a second collection of short stories and a novel.

Joy Sotolongo lives in Durham, North Carolina, and has an M.A. in Rehabilitation Administration from De Paul University. She works for a local family support program and writes for *Carolina Parent*.

Sally Sullivan, a professor in the Department of English at the University of North Carolina at Wilmington, has published poems, short stories and textbooks.

Jamie Tevis, a native of Kentucky, is retired and has published articles in *Kentucky Review* and the *Richmond Register*. She is host of a cable-access television show.

Leslie Tompkins lives in Charlotte, North Carolina, where she works in the Writing Center at Central Piedmont Community College. She has published a chapbook, *Summer Holds Too Long* (1988).

Katerina Whitley, a native of Thessaloniki, Greece, has lived in the South for twenty-seven years. She is the editor of *Lifeline*, a publication of the Presiding Bishop's Fund for World Relief, where she is also a public relations associate.

Amy Wilson holds a B.A. and an M.A. in Literature and has worked as a feature writer and journalist.

Wilma Wilson is a designer and writer who states, "One pays the bills, one lights my days; both make my spirit soar when that which was only in the mind become reality."

Maggie Wynne lives in Raleigh, North Carolina. Currently she is using family letters as a basis for a writing project about her grandmother, her great-grandmother, and her great-great-grandmother.